KEVIN KEEGAN

KEVIN KEEGAN

Kevin Keegan

READERS UNION
Group of Book Clubs
Newton Abbot 1978

First published by Arthur Barker Limited

This edition was produced in 1978 for sale to its members
only by the proprietors, Readers Union Limited,
PO Box 6, Newton Abbot, Devon, TQ12 2DW.
Full details of membership will gladly be sent on request

Reproduced and printed in Great Britain
by A. Wheaton & Co Limited Exeter
for Readers Union

Contents

IN MEMORY OF MY FATHER

Foreword

This book presents many vivid illustrations, from the dust-jacket onwards, of Kevin Keegan's impetuous style of football: busy body, tongue thrusting, eyes on the ball, mind on the next move but one; boundless energy and fearless, almost frenetic determination. It is surprising that a young man in such a hurry should have taken so long to arrive.

Kevin was three months into his twentieth year when Liverpool bought him from Scunthorpe United for a modest £33,000 ('Robbery with violence' was Bill Shankly's phrase in retrospect) in 1971. That in itself should provide ample encouragement for those who have faith in their ability to succeed, at whatever, and crave an opportunity. But to fully appreciate the significance of Kevin's slow germination it is necessary to bear in mind the evolution of the game from the 1950s.

Matt Busby, manager of Manchester United, and Stan Cullis, manager of Wolverhampton Wanderers, two former half backs of style and imagination, conceived that it would be more practicable and profitable to create their own nurseries for young players than to follow the traditional dependence upon smaller clubs to feed the transfer market. Soon club talent scouts scoured Britain's playgrounds for prodigious adolescents and the football factories flourished.

The system was thorough, the catches were enormous and players who missed the nets were as rare as cod swimming from Billingsgate. Gradually, the catches began to diminish, in quantity and quality, which made it all the more remarkable that so many experienced anglers should have chosen to ignore Kevin in his small pond.

It is easy to express such thoughts now, of course, but I must own up to the fact that when I first saw a match in which Kevin played I never even noticed him. The sequence of events leading up to that oblivious encounter began on 17 September 1968, when I travelled to Spain with Liverpool to report their European Fairs Cup first round match against Atletico Bilbao for the *Daily Express*. Liverpool lost that first leg of the tie 2–1 (winning the return match 2–1 at Anfield the following month but being knocked out on the spin of a disc when scores were level on aggregate after extra time). The trip stuck in my mind for two reasons. When the airplane arrived back at Speke, Noel Cantwell was waiting to sign centre forward Tony Hateley for Coventry City for £80,000 (Shankly then turned his attention towards Wolves and made 18-year-old Alun Evans Britain's first £100,000 teenage footballer) and half the passengers, including myself, were about to be stricken with diarrhoea.

I was still in the grip of Spanish Revenge five days later when I was assigned to

7

cover a third round Football League Cup tie between Fourth Division Scunthorpe and First Division Arsenal. People usually pass *through* Scunthorpe, which is a pity, because the town has strived to live down an image marginally less exotic than that evoked by the very mention of Wigan. Comedian Jimmy Edwards made an apology in North Lincolnshire after saying, in reference to somewhere else 'Orrible place. Like Scunthorpe on a Sunday morning.' But when Councillor Hamilton Spencer was mayor of the municipal borough in 1952 he had no town hall and told *Yorkshire Post* correspondent Derrick Boothroyd, 'We call ourselves the dead-end kids here in Scunthorpe. When we put our robes on we can't help thinking that they're worth more than all our public buildings put together.' One hundred years ago Scunthorpe was an agricultural village of 616 inhabitants, but when iron ore was discovered industry imposed on nature and the pastoral scene was obscured by a 'boom town' of steel.

The town's football club has not boomed often. The team was nicknamed The Knuts until an unfortunate transposition in a newspaper prompted a swift change to The Irons. In the early 1960s the Rev. David Mansfield, minister of Scunthorpe Baptist Church, offered to become the club's chaplain and suggested that a few prayers might not go amiss at half time.

Arsenal attracted a hopeful congregation of 17,450 to the Old Show Ground and in my preview to the match I wrote that a man on loan and an apprentice figured prominently in Scunthorpe's plans. Ian Davidson, borrowed for three months from Hull City, was almost certain to appear in the number four jersey and ... 'Kevin Keegan, 17, stands by for a spot in the forward line and the most nerve-racking test of his life.'

Scunthorpe were beaten 6–1 and I wrote of how the Lincolnshire heavens had opened and Scunthorpe's courageous effort had dripped slowly but surely down the drain. I described the goals and wrote about sundry incidents. But I did not mention Kevin Keegan ... though he insists he played! I can only put my oversight down to the Bilbao bug.

When next I saw Kevin he was Liverpool's latest signing and was lost in the post-Wembley depression of the 1971 FA Cup Final, when Liverpool were beaten 2–1 by Arsenal in extra time. He stood, dark, smart and quiet, with his girl friend, Jean, on a platform at Euston Station as people bustled in search of seats on the train which was to take the players and officials back to Liverpool. Kevin was too new to feel a part of what was happening and had yet to wear the red jersey with the Liver Bird badge and hear the Kop glorify his name.

We could not have known it at the time, but the boy with little to say for himself was the most important player in the club's immediate future, perhaps the most important player in Liverpool's history. As the train was leaving Euston, so Kevin Keegan was arriving. Since then his story has fascinated the football followers of Europe.

Characteristically, every symbol of Kevin's success, trophies, medals and international caps, were handed with boyish pride to his greatest fan: his father, Joe, who died shortly before Christmas, 1976, as Liverpool were in the midst of their most demanding season.

I spent a memorable day with Joe, a retired Geordie miner of Irish (Roscommon) stock, who told me about Kevin's grandfather, Frank Keegan, a hero of the West Stanley pit disaster of 16 February 1909. The disaster claimed the lives of 168 men and boys but, thanks to local inspector Frank and fellow rescuers, thirty men and a pony survived. Joe recited a verse of tribute from that time.

> ... Although just rescued from the mine,
> Frank Keegan turned a rescuer,
> He thought not of his own escape,
> But of his fellow hewer.
> Was duty ever nobler done?
> Was the VC ever nobler won?

Joe's friend, Harry Wadsley, called, as he often did, to drive the old man from his home at Wadworth, Doncaster, to a favourite pub on the outskirts of Rotherham for lunchtime refreshment. During the journey Harry played a cassette recording of Liverpool's 1974 FA Cup Final triumph against Newcastle United.

The two men knew the commentary by heart and their excitement increased as the tape reeled on. I was convinced that they expected Liverpool to win by a wider margin than 3–0 and that Kevin would at least score a double hat-trick.

Where late developers are concerned, I suppose all things are possible.

John Roberts
June 1977

ACKNOWLEDGEMENTS

Illustrations are reproduced by kind permission of the following (by page numbers):

Kevin Keegan 6, 20, 33, 35, 49, 86; Harry Ormesher 10 (*below right*), 53 (*below right*), 73, 76 (*top*), 97, 107 (*below*), 112, 115 (*top & bottom*), 120 (*below*), 125, 126, 130 (*below*), 134, 136, 137, 139 (*top & below right*), 146, 147; *Daily Express* 10 (*top & below left*), 53 (*top & below left*), 76 (*below*), 102 (*top*), 107 (*top*), 130 (*top*), 139 (*below left*); *Daily Mirror* 58, 89 (*below*), 120 (*top*), 121, 152 (*top*); *The Sun* 84 (*below*); H. Goodwin 84 (*top*); County Press Wigan 102 (*below*), 115 (*middle*).

My goal against St Etienne.

Eye on the ball in Zurich.

A visit from Alick Jeffrey.

Symbols of success.

1

The reasons why

'Kevin's football must be encouraged'
– *Sister Mary Oliver*, Headmistress,
St Francis Xavier's Junior School,
Balby Bridge, Doncaster, 1961

Not many footballers have been discovered by a nun, and when s.v. Hamburg paid Liverpool £500,000 for my transfer on 3 June 1977, I wondered if Sister Mary Oliver had realized what she was starting when she wrote that message in my school report. A world of change has taken place in my life since then, but I think it is significant that I have not forgotten my Headmistress's words. The importance of encouragement is one of the themes of my story.

I must begin by endeavouring to explain to those who gave me such wonderful support in England exactly why I moved to West Germany. There are several reasons, some major and some minor.

On 30 March 1976, when Liverpool played the first leg of their UEFA Cup Semi-Final at the Nou Camp Stadium, Barcelona, my thoughts took shape. I looked around at the dressing-rooms, which were almost as big as Liverpool's training ground at Melwood, at the chapel, the magnificent surface of the pitch and the crowd of 85,000. 'What a place!' I thought to myself.

I realized, at that moment, that football in England was one thing, but this was quite another. Suddenly my eyes were opened. Liverpool were the cream of English football. I loved the club and its supporters, and I loved playing for England. But I felt envious of the Barcelona players, and this did not lessen when I heard that Johan Cruyff was about to sign a new contract worth ten thousand pounds a week.

Liverpool won 1–0 (we went on to beat Bruges in the Final) and I made the goal for John Toshack. After we had left the field, elated by our performance, I became conscious that I was not fulfilling myself. I was ambitious, so why shouldn't I aim for the very top, both financially and for my own personal satisfaction? This may seem blasé, but I considered I had already achieved what I wanted in England. There was not much left for me to win. I had no great urge to win a League Cup medal, because, in my view, it is only a secondary competition.

As events turned out, Liverpool went on to win the League Championship again, ensuring them another attempt at the European Cup. That is why I stayed another season and did not push too hard for the move. It also explains why the club was so understanding about the situation.

After the game in Barcelona some of the English press boys came over for a chat and I expressed my feelings about playing abroad. I knew what I was doing. I wanted a new challenge; a new scene with new faces. I was not so stupid as to want to go anywhere else in England, where I would have gained little financially and ended up in a similar rut. It had to be Spain, West Germany or, perhaps, Italy.

I wanted the public, especially in Liverpool, to know from the start that I was keen to go, because it would take a certain amount of pressure off the club. I wanted people to get used to the idea that I would be leaving at the end of the following season; then there would be no reason for the fans to ask the club why I had been sold. As a matter of fact, before long most people were saying, 'Don't stand in his way.'

Having then hinted that I would like to go abroad, the following summer I said I definitely intended to go, and this time Liverpool backed me up. Many people took it for granted that my contract was due to end after the 1976–77 season. In fact, I would not have been free then, because Liverpool still had the option of a further year of my services, but the Chairman, John Smith, and the manager, Bob Paisley, were able to see my point of view. They realized that a move for me would also be in their best interests, and the series of events about which you will read later began to unfold.

I can almost hear people saying that 'he's only gone for the money,' and, though I place ambition above all else, I cannot deny that the financial side of the move was a strong attraction. I had reached the point where, because of taxation, there was no incentive for me to go any further in England. It is no coincidence that other players, like Everton's Bob Latchford, for instance, have struggled financially. We do not expect public sympathy, but it annoys professional footballers when people assume that they are earning large fortunes. They think we can play for ten years, then retire and never work again, but this is just not so.

At first climbing the ladder is exciting, because we live in a society which thankfully does not feel it is wrong to better oneself – up to a point. The early rewards bring a few problems, but it is possible to continue climbing. Then it becomes noticeable how much the government is taking, although ambition still drives one on to the next rung.

I started off at Scunthorpe United, where I was proud simply to be a professional footballer. My initial aim was to play in the first team. Having achieved that, my next goal was to play in a higher grade. I was not necessarily thinking in terms of the First Division, but Liverpool came along, and my ambition was then to justify the fee of £33,000 they had paid for me. I was fortunate to win a place in the first team quickly, and was determined to help the club win more trophies. Before long I was playing for the England Under-23 team, after which my goal became the senior international team, and so on.

The financial rewards kept pace with my ambitions, until one day I looked at my tax deductions and wondered what hope there was in the future. The manager wanted to give me a rise, but I did not want it. It was worth nothing to me. I have a limited company, so not all my time has been spent hitting my head against a wall. On the contrary, I have done very well, earning twice as much from advertising and endorsements as from football.

Few players are as fortunate as I have been, and footballers are as guilty as anyone of establishing lifestyles beyond their means. Even when earning twenty thousand pounds a year, they overlook the fact that after the tax man has taken his share they will be left with about eleven thousand. In England, successful people are encouraged by the system to try all kinds of legal fiddles to ease their tax problems and get their hands on more of the money they have earned. People may say, 'I wish I were paying your tax', but that does not make the system fair.

I was criticized for driving a Japanese car, while being captain of England, but I still had a living to make in a short period of time. If I didn't have the brains to accept the kind of deal I was offered for my Datsun compared with one for a home-produced model then I would not have deserved the England captaincy!

I'm not mean, but I don't throw money around. There is no bottomless pocket in which to dip my hand, and though I am optimistic in many ways, I accept that one day I may have to count the pennies more than I do now.

A great deal of money was invested in my home in North Wales. My wife, Jean, and I put a lot of time, thought and effort into the house – I took enormous pleasure in working on it myself – and we had to sacrifice what we had built together in order to make the move. If I am going to give something up, I want something in return. If I am going to have to suffer pressure and take knocks, I want the necessary financial reward. If I am going to have aggravation, I want to know that there is some compensation at the bank.

Money is important, but other, more personal, factors have also contributed to my decision.

It annoys me slightly when people ask, 'Don't you think you owe Liverpool something?' I do not owe them anything, neither do they owe me anything. I gave them complete commitment in every game I played over six years. In most games this helped the team towards winning one point, two points or a cup-tie. Sometimes I had an off day, when nothing worked out right. But how can you owe something when you have given everything?

Liverpool owe me nothing, because they always treated me well, from the moment they gambled by signing me to the conclusion of the deal that took me abroad. They are a great club, respected throughout the world. They have earned that respect, but no organization is perfect and it would be wrong for me to pretend that I was happy with everything that happened at Anfield.

The essence of Bill Shankly's teaching was, 'Look after the little things and the big things will look after themselves,' but the club sometimes fell down on what he taught them. Shanks himself was among those who suffered. I believe he should have been given a throne in the middle of the Directors' Box at Anfield, and the bitterness that developed between him and the club was a source of great disappointment to me. It was not all one-sided because Shanks was not blameless for what happened, but there was one particular example of pettiness that disgusted me. A couple of years after he retired as manager, the club invited Shanks to travel with them to Bruges for the second leg of the UEFA Cup Final. It was a good gesture to make at a time when the relationship between Shanks and the club was strained. But they then went and spoiled it all by booking him into a hotel with the players' wives instead of keeping him with the official party. They made him feel as if he was not wanted.

I know Liverpool is a big club, and the bigger any club grows the harder it is to keep tabs on everything, but it is sad when little humanitarian touches are overlooked. Whatever I did, I could never have done half as much for Liverpool as Shanks, and I knew that they could have turned round and treated me even worse than him. They dealt with certain other players shabbily, in my view.

When a player is out of the team for one reason or another and struggling, he needs encouragement. First team players are usually happy, because they are in the swing of things, but a player who has lost his way needs extra help. At Liverpool there seemed to be a tendency to ignore players in this position which I could never understand.

When I went to Liverpool I kept hearing about John McLaughlin. All the other players rated him highly, believing that, at nineteen, he would become an important part of the foundations of the new team. Managers, coaches and supporters may rave about a player but when his team mates praise him it is worth taking notice, because they are the ones who really know.

My first impression of Johnny was that he lacked pace, but I soon noticed his good points – the way he used the ball so well, rarely giving it away and usually finding a team mate with an accurate pass from midfield, and his cool temperament. Johnny never seemed to be flustered, unlike so many current English footballers – and I am as guilty as any other – who want to go everywhere too quickly, always looking for short cuts, forgetting that sometimes the best way to goal is the long way and that patience can bring rewards.

He was a very patient lad, who had begun to establish himself in the team when I made my debut. Johnny was the sort of player spectators would accept when things were going well, but tended to turn against when the team found difficulty in making headway. Being neither quick nor hard, Johnny could not change the course of a game that was going against his team. He suddenly lost his place in the first team and was out for a year, subsequently returning for the odd game, only to keep missing out again. I could sense he was slipping away. Once the heart is taken out of a player then the rest follows.

All the early talk of success led Johnny to expect a great deal of his career, but he was shy, reserved and rarely said very much, which did not help him. It was obvious when I had been at Anfield for a year that Johnny was no longer regarded as first team material, and clubs from lower divisions began making enquiries about him. Liverpool held on to him, just in case, which is what they always tend to do. They did not like to lose players who could still step into the team when necessary. That was fair enough, from the club's point of view. But what about the player's career? Players have been criticized for showing no loyalty to their clubs, but it cuts both ways. Eventually, Johnny received a bad knee injury. I met him again early in 1977, when he was twenty-five years old and on the dole in Liverpool. That made me think. Once again I was seeing the other face of football.

I admit to a certain prejudice towards Peter Cormack. He was my closest friend at Liverpool; we roomed together and could almost read each other's minds. I have heard it said that I was the last piece in Shanks's jigsaw when he rebuilt the team, but I think Peter was that important piece, because he had the ability to change Liverpool's pattern of play with one telling pass. Peter had a cartilage operation towards the end of the 1974-75 season. His period of recovery took place during the close season, which was unfortunate for him because though he trained he had no way of knowing how fit he was until he could have match practice. The hard work immediately pre-season took its toll on Peter's knee and set him back a little. This was no one's fault, in particular, but again there was a lack of encouragement from the club.

Peter's confidence would have been boosted if he had been taken on one of the club's European trips, if only to be made to feel that he was still part of the squad. But this did not happen. One moment a player is in the team and everything is going well, then before he knows it he is struggling in the reserves.

I tried to console Peter, but it was not easy. 'You'll get back, just keep going,' I would say. 'Get yourself fit. Work hard. Things will work out.' The problem was that Peter's eagerness to get back into the team had done his knee no good. Ray Kennedy had taken his place and the team was on its way to winning the League Championship and the UEFA Cup. The circumstances were against him, because Bob Paisley could not lose face with the players who had come into the team and had done a good job for him, just to make Peter feel better.

A similar thing happened to Larry Lloyd. He was injured, Phil Thompson was pushed into the back four in what seemed to be a panic move, and it came off as one of the best ever positional switches. Larry became frustrated. He did not want reserve team football, which was understandable, because he was the best 'stopper' in England at the time, and consequently was transferred to Coventry.

Football is a man's game, and I am not trying to soften it. It is ruthless. If you win you are everything and if you lose you are nothing, and when a group of players are battling for places life is bound to become a little nasty from time to time. Peter felt he was good enough to be in the first team. He could have stayed at Liverpool and earned good money, but he was not content to do that, and so he moved to Bristol City.

In a sense, I think Peter was a victim of the modern game. He was always willing to hit three passes forward hoping one would get through and make a goal, whereas too many midfield players hit three square passes and are happy to know they are not risking giving the ball to the opposition. Certain players hate to take on responsibility. Every pass they make is a 'safe' pass. They don't think, 'There's a chance I might get the ball through and if I don't, well, it's unlucky.' They think, 'Oh, I won't try that. Someone might cut it out.' I do not have much time for that kind of player – he simply makes up the numbers, robot fashion. As a forward, I found Peter a wonderful player to have in midfield, because the attacking passes are the ones that bring the goals.

One player who, more than any other, helped me to establish myself at Liverpool was Alec Lindsay, the left back. Alec's long passing of the ball with his left foot was so accurate that when I made a run I knew exactly how and where the ball would be flighted, giving me the yard start I needed on any defender. To Alec, I was a moving target. He had a knack of finding me with the ball, and if he'd had a particularly good game I would point to my chest and say, 'There it is again, Alec – "Mitre" spelt backwards. You've hit me so often that the trade mark has been transferred from the ball to me.' If ever Alec chipped a ball upfield and missed me, I would stare at him in disbelief.

One of the best – or worst – things Alec did for me was to change the direction of my play. When I came to Liverpool I was a right-sided player, but within a year I could only play on the left side. Alec was so accurate that I used to depend upon his passes. We developed a pattern – something that has been missing from English football recently – whereby Alec would hit the ball upfield for me to run on to, and I would have Steve Heighway out wide, Peter Cormack behind and John Toshack moving on towards the middle. It gave me several alternatives for the next move and kept the other team guessing.

When Alec dropped out of the team these alternatives were drastically reduced, and it took a while for me to adapt to the change of style. The team was still good enough to win major honours, but I found it a world of difference playing in front of Joey Jones. Joey is loved by the lads on the Kop, being a real character, the type of fellow everyone takes to straight away, but I sometimes found his play frustrating in contrast to Alec's. He was a far better tackler and also faster, but he lacked Alec's finesse. One out of every three of Joey's passes went into touch, another would go over my head and, if I was lucky, one would find its way through to me.

Whoever I play for during the rest of my career, I doubt that I will ever come across a better full back than the Alec Lindsay who played for England when Joe Mercer was in charge. Then Alec had domestic problems and his form began to suffer. He lost his place in the team and, just when he needed help most, he became one of the forgotten men. He became increasingly depressed until one day, when we were returning from Melwood on the club bus, he said, 'I'm cheesed off with the game.'

'How do you mean, cheesed off?' I asked, knowing that Alec had been playing in a five-a-side game with the reserves and the youngsters.

'I'm just sick of football. I have fallen out of love with it. To be honest with you, if Real Madrid were playing Bayern Munich in my back garden, I'd draw the curtains.'

It made a pleasant change some time later to hear Alec singing 'Do you know the way to San José?' He had received an offer to play there during the English close season, and was genuinely pleased for the first time in two years. He looked upon the trip to America as a new start, and was so lifted by it that he talked of little else. The best part was his change of attitude. He told me, 'I'll go over there. I want to play and I'll feel wanted. Then I'll come back here next season and I'll get my place back, because I still believe I'm the best left back at the club.' When Alec went to sort out the details with Liverpool, however, he was told that if he was going to play in America they would want a fee of £3000. That put paid to Alec's trip and knocked the lad down again, which I thought was a pretty small-minded thing for Liverpool to do. What was £3000 to them?

Chris Lawler's tragedy touched us all. While we did not spend our time having tea at each other's houses, we were still a fairly close knit team on and off the field, and we pulled together when someone was having a bad time. When Chris's little daughter was killed in an accident in his garden, there was very little we could do for him except feel deeply sorry. The club offered to give Chris a free transfer and pay him what was due from the remaining year of his contract. The players thought that a year's wages plus the chance to move and negotiate new terms elsewhere was very generous. It was the sort of treatment Chris deserved, because he had done a marvellous job for Liverpool.

No full back scored as many goals as Chris – amazingly, none came from penalties – and though he was not particularly good in the tackle, lacked a bit of pace and was unbelievably quiet, he was never given the run around and always managed to move up to the edge of the box, looking for goals. He was still capable of first team football, but was beginning to lose his edge when Phil Neal arrived and took over at right back. It was a good time all round for Chris to make a move.

Southport and Stockport were both keen to sign him, and he was thinking over their offers when Manchester City said they would take him for a year as cover for their full back positions. That seemed an excellent opportunity for Chris to join another top-class club, perhaps play a few first team games, and then move down a division or two later. Chris told Liverpool he had decided to go to Manchester City, but the club told Chris that if a First Division club was involved they would want a fee of £20,000. This hurt the other players, because once Chris had been offered a 'free' it should not have mattered where he went, whether it was Rochdale or Real Madrid. A move to City would have been a dream for Chris, but, having given him a present, Liverpool took it back again.

Chris eventually moved to Portsmouth, but the bitterness of what happened to him lingered on with me. It made it easier for me to leave, because it was another example of how things can work against a player when the boot is on the other foot. It hammered home the message that life is about the survival of the strongest and the fittest.

A man who does not know what he is worth is not worth anything, and I knew what I was worth to Liverpool. I also knew that whatever happened, Liverpool were not going to lose. At worst, they would make a lot of money by selling me, and no one is indispensable. All kinds of people told me that I was mad to want to leave Liverpool, the best team in England with the best supporters in the world. What more could I possibly desire? I wanted a fresh challenge. I wanted to prove that not only could Kevin Keegan play top-class football in England, but he could also play top-class football abroad – and, perhaps, win more medals.

In some ways I envy Ian Callaghan and in other ways I don't. I like Cally and respect him for his attitude and the 800 games he has played for Liverpool. Occasionally I have thought that it would be good to be like Cally and settle for a career with one club, but to do this I would have to wear blinkers and keep going along the one course.

This is not for me. If I had been told that I would still be at Liverpool five years from now, it would have been like having a sword pushed through my heart. I became depressed because I felt I had done all I could for Liverpool. Only Jean knows how hard it was for me to keep going when my heart and soul was no longer in the club. What used to be an incredible experience did not quite mean the same any more and was becoming a very hard struggle. I was only looking forward to the end of the season, so I could move away and start afresh.

People eventually accepted that I was leaving, and while that was a good thing it also had its disadvantages. I began to feel that some of the supporters were turning against me. When a substitution was about to be made, I sensed that some people wanted me to be brought off, although I cannot be sure whether that was simply a psychological reaction on my part. Feeling the way I did, it was only fair to the supporters who stuck by me that I should leave, having done the best I could for them. The last thing I wanted was a gradual winding down of an association that had been both satisfying and successful.

Other English players – Duncan McKenzie being the most publicized example – have failed to make a lasting impression on the Continent in recent years, so what makes me think I can succeed? When McKenzie was transferred from Leeds United to Anderlecht, I said I would be surprised if he made it over there, and I am not being wise after the event. I cannot deny that he has skill, and the fans love him because he is an entertainer. He is fun to have around. But his record of consistency is not good. At Leeds he played three or four good games out of ten. He was unable to string together six, seven or eight useful performances. If he was unable to command a place at Leeds, why was it taken for granted by some people that he would fit into a successful Belgian side?

It was argued that McKenzie's style was better suited to Continental football. The approach to the game does vary a little from country to country, but generally, throughout the world, the player who involves himself as much as possible in every game will always be better than one who drifts in and out of matches.

If someone said I was the greatest player in England, I would not accept it, because I know it isn't true. But if they said that in the last five or even ten years no player in England had played as consistently well as I had, I would not argue. My off days have been few and far between and my play is never short of effort. I honestly believe I can make it, and, though I was a little surprised at the amount of money paid for me and the number of clubs who were keen to sign me, I knew that nobody was rushing out blind to buy me. They had studied my play for a year or two before deciding that given a fair chance and a bit of luck, I would be a great asset.

The English League is the hardest league in the world. None of the forty-two games is easy, because the level of ability and competition is more even than anywhere else. In addition, there are all the cup matches and the ground conditions which vary considerably over the nine months of the season. Elsewhere, football seems to be dominated by an elite of clubs, with smaller divisions and fewer really tough matches. If a player has shown consistent form in England, he must have a chance of doing well abroad.

I knew I was putting myself under pressure, but that is what I needed if I was to achieve something. I was brought up to be appreciative, however, and experience has taught me to keep my feet on the ground. Although I am only twenty-six, I have already seen many sides of life and have not forgotten where I came from.

The miner's son.

2

The miner's son

My dad, Joe, was a Geordie miner who moved to Yorkshire when work was scarce on the Durham seams. He came to Markham Main Colliery and I was born at Elm Place in the village of Armthorpe in February 1951. My first real memories are of growing up in the heart of Doncaster. There is a modern shopping precinct in the centre of Doncaster and the ABC cinema now stands on what used to be my back garden, where I first learnt how to control a football.

Number 25 Spring Gardens was in a row of terraced houses, something like television's Coronation Street; the sort of place that is regarded as a slum. That type of housing has been replaced by high-rise flats – concrete in the skies! At least we had gardens, and ours, long and narrow, with lilac bushes down one side and a big brick wall down the other, provided a playing area large enough for six or seven kids. The wall, without windows, was built on to Mrs Wild's house next door and was ideal for the continual thudding of a ball as we kicked or headed it, making believe we were Wolverhampton Wanderers playing one of the foreign teams in matches we had seen on television. I always wanted to be Billy Wright, the Wolves and England captain.

In the middle of the garden was the toilet, at least twenty yards away from the house and without windows as a result of our games of football. One bonfire night, Dad was sitting on the toilet. One of my friends lit a 'Jumping Jack' and I threw it through the space where the window used to be. 'You buggers! Wait till I get hold of you!' shouted my father. I can remember running away in case I got a smack on the backside or a clip round the ear. Once I dropped a brick down the toilet bowl (I cannot recall why) and caused considerable damage. I told my Mum, Doris, and she helped me to stick it together again somehow. But next time Dad pulled the chain, water and muck gushed all over his shoes. Fortunately they were his brown shoes!

When I discovered that Dad worked underground I imagined that if I dug far enough down in the garden, I would meet him in the pit. In no time the garden was scarred with my potholes, and whenever I got under Mum's feet, she would say, 'Why don't you go and look for your Dad?'

We had a detached outhouse, with broken windows and slates missing from the roof, where we washed. There was a boiler in the corner, where Mum washed our clothes and a sink where we washed ourselves. We had a tin bath tub and, from the boiling of the water on the gas rings to towelling down, bathing took two or three hours.

The house itself had a front room, which we rarely used, a small hall with stairs leading to a couple of bedrooms, and a kitchen/dining area. Mary, my sister, is two years older than I but we were young enough to share the same room. Mike, my brother, who is seven years younger than I, was in his cot in the front bedroom with Mum and Dad. There was no front door, but one instead at the side, in an entry we shared with the people next door. Our cellar was far larger than any other room in the house, and we were never short of mice down there. The stairs from the bedrooms to the hall continued down to the cellar, and one night, when I was seven or eight years old and going through a phase of sleepwalking, Mum found me asleep on the coal.

The street was busy and I was fascinated by the trolley-buses, or 'tracklesses' as we called them because they were powered by overhead wires, and did not run on tracks like the trams. In common with most small boys, I loved motor cars, and was a fanatic when it came to collecting the Match Box models made by Lesney. Perhaps it was lucky that we had no front door and I could not run directly out of the house towards the road. Dad told me that when I was four or five Mum had had to run out and pull me off a trackless I had decided to explore. As soon as she got me back to safety, she had fainted.

There was never a dull moment. Two little girls who lived nearby came into our garden one day and we made a see-saw out of a barrel and an old plank. I sat at one end and one of the girls, a dumpy soul, sat at the other. The plank was so rotted that it broke in the centre and a sharp piece of wood hit me under my right eye, leaving a little scar that I still have today.

We lived opposite the Co-op Funeral Service, which was managed by Mr Anderson, the father of David, one of my friends. We often used the big mortuary doors at the side of the building as goals and frequently sneaked inside to have a look at the bodies awaiting burial. We thought nothing of walking around the corpses, even though I would only have been eight and David just three years older.

One day Mr Anderson called to us, 'Come and have a look – it's Father Christmas and he's died.' David and I stopped playing our game, looked at each other, not knowing what to say, and went inside. Mr Anderson took us over to one of the bodies, the remains of a fellow with a long, white beard, who looked very much like the Father Christmas my Mum had taken me to see at one of the big stores. I had reached the age when I was beginning to wonder about Father Christmas. Was there such a person? Mr Anderson said that was him lying there, dead. I remember David and I were very upset about losing such a good friend.

Maurice Freedman was my other pal. He was a year older than I and lived on the same side of the road but, like David, Maurice lived in a house that had electricity. I was jealous, because we only had gas and, apart from feeling underprivileged, I got many a clip over the the ear for breaking mantles, which cost about 1s 3d. They were extremely fragile and would disintegrate at the slightest touch.

David and Maurice also had television, but David's mother was quite houseproud and did not like having 'scruffs' in, with the result that the three of us mainly watched television at Maurice's. His dad worked on the railway and also kept chickens in the back garden. I thought the Freedmans must be wealthy, because no one else in the area kept chickens and few could boast of having a twelve-inch Bush television set. The programmes I remember from those days were 'Torchy', the little battery boy, and 'Bill and Ben', the Flowerpot Men, but it was football that captivated us, especially the big matches televised from Wolverhampton. Wolves became my team in the same way that Liverpool and other top clubs attract boys today. Television brings into people's homes teams that they may never have the chance to see live. I marvelled at players like Wright, Finlayson, Hancocks, Deeley, Broadbent, Flowers, Clamp, Mason and Mullen.

My Uncle Frank, Dad's brother, brought me my first leather football, size five with a lace, but I was puzzled because it had Frank written on when my name was Joseph – Joseph Kevin Keegan. Joseph after my Dad, who died in December 1976, aged seventy-one, but who lived long enough to share some of my proudest moments in spite of a protracted illness. He was much older than Mum. Apart from war service in Burma he spent a lifetime in the mines. In my imagination I can see him now, coming home to Spring Gardens and placing his wages on the table for Mary and I to count the pound notes. I shall never forget the first weekend he came home with five-pound notes in the packet. He just put four down and it looked nothing. He used to hide our pocket money and when we got up on Friday mornings we had to find it – pennies, threepenny bits and, if we were lucky, sixpences. If we had a half-crown we were rich, and I can remember my first ten-shilling note, obtained in exchange for four half-crowns I had saved.

Smoking, drinking and gambling seemed to be the three main pursuits a miner would indulge in to make his hard life a little more bearable. Dad liked a drink and a bet. When I was a kid he would take me with him everywhere except the pub. I often went with him to the betting shop, and used to say we were going to the 'gee-gees'.

Mum and Dad had tiffs, as every married couple does, but I cannot remember their having a serious argument. Dad was not a drunkard, but he loved his beer, which was not surprising considering how much of his time was spent in the mines. Occasionally, he would drink too much. On one such day, I was in the kitchen, when suddenly I heard a thumping noise and my Mum shouting, 'You bugger, you're drunk, don't come home like this again!' She was holding his ears and banging his head against the wall outside. Of course, he had had so much to drink that he didn't even feel it!

On another occasion, Mum decided to teach him a lesson. He came home drunk and promptly fell asleep. Dad's hair had been snow-white since he was twenty-one. He used to say it was caused by the soap at the mine but I think it was just the way he was made. While he was in the deep sleep of the drunk, Mum dyed his hair jet-black. Next morning when Dad looked in the mirror, he had a white moustache and black hair. He shaved off the moustache and set off for work. On the bus he sat next to his mate, a man who had known him for many years. This man stared at him for some time, until finally my Dad said, 'What's wrong with you?'

'I know you are a Keegan,' said his friend. 'I know Frank and Joe – he is my best mate – but who are you?'

'Bugger off or I'll hit you!' replied Dad. 'It *is* Joe. The wife did this.'

It took some six months for the dye to grow out of Dad's hair, which turned green and then blue before finally returning to snow-white again.

Mike had not been at school very long when he brought home an essay, which turned out to be a family character reading: 'My Dad is fifty. My Dad backs horses. My Dad drinks beer and gets drunk. My Dad shouts at my Mum.' Mum fared rather better: 'My Mum is twenty-one [she was about forty at the time]. She is beautiful. She is good. Dad sometimes shouts at her.'

When Dad had been for a drink he would occasionally give us extra pocket money and he never failed, whether or not he had had a drink, to bring us something; such as chocolate, peanuts, crisps and pop. He never came home empty handed. Drink can be good for people, as long as they know when they have had enough. I could always tell when Dad had had one or two over his limit. He would take the mickey out of me, saying, 'You big-nosed bugger' and that sort of thing. But there was never any harm in him. He never wanted to fight or do anything else silly. Towards the end of his life, he could only manage half-a-pint, because of his illness, and I felt sad about that. I wish he were getting drunk now.

My parents were two of the best fives and three domino players in Doncaster, but Dad said the worst thing he ever did was to teach Mum how to play because it improved her ability to count. When he had a win on the horses he could not hide money from her because she could work out the odds quicker than he could.

Whenever Mum was working, which depended upon Dad's state of health, Mary was given the responsibility of keeping the house clean and, during the school holidays, I had to look after Mike. It proved something of a drawback, because I had to drag him along everywhere and at one stage I became so fed up with him that I could not stand to be near him. Whatever I wanted to do, Mum would say, 'If you want to go, take Mike.' It was like having a dog on a lead, but, although I thought he was a nuisance then, we became very close later and I do not see as much of him now as I would like to.

I used to take Mike to Hyde Park, which was about a mile and a half from where we lived, and when my friends and I played football we would put a coat down for one goal-post and use Mike in his pram as the other. Many a time the ball whacked him in the face, and when we went home he would say, 'Mum, our Kevin has used me for a goal-post again.' Another job I was given to prove my existence in the house was toast-watching at breakfast time. Mum would plug in a gas ring, light it and fix the bread to a fork, and then I would keep my eye on it to make sure it did not burn.

Although Dad worked in the mine, he always looked fairly smart. The colliery was a twenty-minute bus ride, and he would not change into his working clothes until he arrived there. Every morning there was a ritual. Dad, who had chronic bronchitis, would start to cough. Shortly after, a loud barking sound would come from outside at the back of the house and Dad would say, 'Big Banger's off again.' Big Banger was a massive fellow who lived in Baker Street, his backyard being behind ours. He also had a cough, and Dad would set him off. They would go on for ten minutes or quarter-of-an-hour. Dad told me the story of 'Jack and the Beanstalk' and when I looked down towards the bottom of our garden my imagination would start to work. There was a big lilac tree, which I imagined to be the beanstalk. In the distance there was an office block with a slanting roof, and that became the castle. When Big Banger was about, usually in a white vest and trousers, he was so enormous that I could see his head and shoulders above the wall. He was the giant, and even though he didn't say 'Fe, fi, fo fum,' Big Banger still made plenty of noise.

Mrs Wild lived to one side of us and our other next-door neighbour was a character we called 'Old Gibby', Mr Gibbons. Old Gibby seemed to have a grudge against the world and especially against me. His favourite expression was 'kids and bloody cats'. One day I was playing with a balloon, which stuck in a tree. I tried to dislodge it by throwing stones. At first I tossed the stones gently, but this had no effect, so I threw one very hard which flew into the tree and through Old Gibby's bedroom window. Fortunately, he was out at the time and Dad knew someone who put windows in. The man knocked out the damaged pane, climbed into the bedroom and cleared the broken glass. When he had finished, Dad touched up the putty with the same colour paint as the frame to make it look right, but there were still a few bits of glass in Old Gibby's bedroom. He was not too pleased about it all.

When I was a kid I just thought Gibby was an old moaner. I later found out that he had lost his wife. He was not too keen on the Keegans from the time he went on holiday and asked Dad to look after his dog. He thought the world of that dog, but Spring Gardens was an awful place to keep a dog and, while Dad was keeping an eye on me, toddling about with Mary, the dog wandered on to the road and was run over.

Dad was not a do-it-yourself expert. On one occasion when we had moved house, the bathroom cabinet fell off the wall. 'Come here, son, and hold this,' he said, and used the longest nail I had ever seen to put it up again. Our next door neighbour came round to say Dad had knocked all the panels off his wall. The nail had gone right through, and we used to joke that on one side it held up our cabinet and on the other side the fellow next door hung up his towel.

I tried my hand at everything. When I was nine Dad was very ill and he and Mary went to convalesce at an aunt's hotel in Llandudno. While they were away my mother and I papered and painted the downstairs of the house. I put the paste on the paper and would hold it, while Mum climbed the ladder. I was decorating the house on my own by the age of twelve, though once I did become slightly over-ambitious. We bought some polystyrene edging to make a neat job between the ceiling and the walls; enough to do the whole room, but it was expensive and I told Mum not to worry about special pieces for the corner. I thought I could cut the angles myself with a knife, not realizing that a machine would be needed. By the time I finished there was only three feet of polystyrene left, and the angle was still not right.

Mum has been a grafter all her life and, when she could, she liked to go out to work. One year, Dad did not work at all because of bronchitis and Mum took all kinds of jobs, including cleaning at a pub. My parents taught me to work for things, and I hate getting something for nothing. I never appreciate anything unless it has cost me some effort. If I have worked hard on one of the commercial contracts that have come my way through football, then I enjoy the money because I know I have earned it. I am neither tight-fisted nor shrewd, but I appreciate the value of money and know that sometimes I can afford to be a little extravagant.

I would do anything for Mum. She worked even when the doctor told her to rest her legs, which are covered with varicose veins. I would kneel down and let her rest her legs on my back, like a cushion. This I would do for an hour at a time, happy to think I was helping out. One of my favourite errands was to take the laundry to the launderette, about two miles from the house. Mum would put it into a pram and say, 'Here is twopence for the washing powder, twopence for the bleach, a penny for the drier and two shillings for the machine.' If the laundry weighed more than eight-and-a-half pounds, I would have to leave some of it out of the machine. The women at the launderette gave me sympathetic looks, and I could hear them say, 'Poor little bugger – what's his mother doing sending him?' I was only as big as the bag, but I loved those trips with the laundry.

I also tried to boost the family income with a few boyhood business ventures. Dave was the brains and Maurice and I were his partners. There was the firewood business. Doncaster market was one of the best in Yorkshire, and we would start our work when the stall holders were finishing theirs. We hunted for wooden boxes, some of which were put in piles and others left in dustbins. Orange boxes were rare, because they were very good boxes. We would take a trolley and stack it up with all the wood we could lay our hands on. Then the real fun began as we pushed the trolley home, a journey of three-quarters of a mile. Passing cars would blow their horns to warn us of the dangers of travelling along the side of the road instead of the pavement, a course we took to avoid the ups-and-downs of moving from pavement to pavement as we crossed from one road to another. Motorists would often have to steer clear of a couple of boxes that had fallen from our load.

We went back and forward from the markets five or six times to search through the bins and collect the boxes. Then we would go into my backyard and chop up the boxes, most of which could be easily broken by hand, and sort the pieces into bundles, secured with wire we had taken from the boxes. Then we went out into Spring Gardens and neighbouring streets, knocking on doors and selling the firewood at twopence a bundle. We did not go all round the block, because there was always a chance that we might run into a gang of lads, older than we were. These ruffians did not like us and would pinch our bundles. We would run away because they were so much bigger than we were. I remember shouting names at them, being caught and clipped round the ear, and then running home crying. I was at the age when you did not stand and fight, you just made sure you ran faster than the others.

Dave, being the oldest and the leader of our group, used to bully me sometimes. He would take advantage of his size, and I would go crying to my father about him. 'Bloody hit him back. Don't come in here crying,' was Dad's reaction. Dave later snatched something off me and, instead of crying, I grabbed it back. When he snatched it off me again, I thumped him on the nose and gave him a good hiding. This time Dave was the one who went home crying.

That night, when Dad was at the Liberal Club, Dave's father told him all about the fight, because he had watched us from his window and could not stop laughing. He thought it was great that I had finally got my own back on his son. When Dad saw me next he said, 'Have you been fighting?'

'No, no.'

'Well, I know you've been fighting. Don't let me ever catch you again, you little bugger,' said Dad. Having been told off for crying and for sticking up for myself, I wondered what to do for the best. I knew that Dad was really pleased for me although he could not say so at the time.

Dave also suggested that we could make money by washing cars. Doncaster is a great horse-racing town, famous for the St Leger, and not far from Spring Gardens were the Glasgow Paddocks, a place the size of eight or nine football pitches, where hundreds of horses were stabled and auctioned. It has now been replaced by the National Coal Board building, police headquarters and a museum, which came as a great blow to Dave, Maurice and myself.

Wealthy people used to go to the Paddocks, and as there were no parking facilities they used to leave their large, expensive cars at the side of the road, which was ideal for us. 'Clean your car, Mister?' we said, and people would think nothing of handing us half-a-crown for our work. They did not pay until they returned from the Paddocks, and we had to sit by the car and wait patiently. This often limited us to washing just three cars a day, though we usually split a pound between us. As with the profits from the firewood, I would tip over the money to my mother.

Unfortunately, our little operation was too good to last. It was decided that the Paddocks would be knocked down and the horse sales re-housed near the racecourse, three miles away, which was too far for us to go with our buckets of water. When the local newspaper got to hear about our sad plight, I gave my second press conference. The paper used a picture of us sitting disconsolately on our buckets. I had then grown accustomed to dealing with the press – the paper had printed a picture of me putting at a local park when I was five!

At the age of seven I told Dad that I would like a newspaper round to earn some money. I was keen to be a little independent. There was a newsagent's shop round the corner from where we lived and, after a great deal of pestering, Dad took me to apply for a job, although it was only to humour me. I was only three feet tall and the woman who ran the shop looked me up and down. 'I know you are a good worker,' she began, which pleased me, 'but do you think you will be able to reach the letterboxes?'

'I'll carry a box round with me,' I replied, believing I had eliminated this problem.

'Well look, will you come back in a couple of years?'

That really hurt me. 'I could do with a job now,' I persisted.

'Come on then,' said the woman, and, together with Dad, she took me down the road for a trial. They must have picked the highest letterbox in Doncaster. It was not a little flat one half-way up the door, but ran longways near the top. I doubt if I could have reached it if I'd had a step ladder. She had proved her point, but promised me a job in a few years' time as a consolation. Dad took me home with my pride hurt. I left the district before I was tall enough to reach that letterbox.

One of the main treats of the year was to be taken to the St Leger fair, during the major race meeting. It was a real family affair and Uncle Frank and Aunt Kitty used to come along with us. We would have ice-cream and if Dad won on the horses we could have just about anything we asked for – but if he had lost we kept quiet or we might get a clip round the ear. I remember running over to the rails to enjoy the marvellous thrill of the horses shooting by. Dad always wanted one to win, but all I could see was the blur of colours and numbers flashing by. I was mad keen about the penny slot-machines, which cost my parents a fortune. I would head for them at the St Leger fair and also when Dad's working men's club in Armthorpe organized day trips to Cleethorpes. I was given 17s 6d spending money and they would be back for me at lunch, by which time I would have spent it all on the one-armed bandits. Dad would tell me off and make me sit on the sand. I used to sulk, because I never wanted to make sand pies or swim like the other kids. I only wanted to play the slot-machines and ride on the dodgems.

I did not like going to school and shortly after I started I had an accident at home. Our stairs were spiral and I fell from top to bottom, bruising my face. Mum took me to a shop, bought me lots of chocolate and a new toy and let me have the day off. Next morning I threw myself down the stairs to wangle another day off, with more chocolate and another toy. I walked half-way down the stairs, gave a little scream and flung myself, out Mum realized what I was up to and, though I was a bit sore from the fall, she spanked me and sent me off to school.

Mum is a Protestant while Dad was Roman Catholic, and it was understood that Mary, Mike and I would be brought up as Catholics. I believe it is a good faith, but, from the start of school, I could sense that it set me apart from many of the people around me. I felt it more when I was young than I do now, because I can now see things in proportion. People say you should not feel different because of your religion, but I think you are meant to feel different. The very thing it stands for is the difference; the fact that you have to trapse across town to go to a Catholic school and get up and go to church on a Sunday morning, when most of your friends are in bed. Where I grew up, Catholics were in a minority. Dave and Maurice, for instance, went to Beechfield, a Protestant school, while I was at St Peter's RC Primary, in Lord Street, near the markets where we went for boxes. I never had any problems from Dave or Maurice, but being a Catholic meant there was always rivalry with kids from Protestant schools.

Religion gave me a base. It taught me about discipline, because I had to go to church on Sunday and, although this should be accepted as the most important part of the week, the effort had to be made to go. I was putting myself out for something I believed in and attempting to live up to the Ten Commandments, teaching right from wrong.

It can be argued that Catholic schools shove religion down pupils' throats, which I suppose many of them do, but schooling sets people up for life. Children from the age of about fifteen start to know their own minds, and a good upbringing can carry them through. My religion was my guideline and I am grateful for it, though I can and I do pick faults in my faith.

Having been friendly with Protestants all my life I am accustomed to their scepticism about the confessional. When I was a child I would go into the box and confess my sins to a priest, all of which would be forgiven – and then I would commit the same sins all over again. How can that be right? I would give up trying to explain, because even priests have difficulty in giving an answer that will satisfy kids, and I used to wonder about it myself. I believe in my religion, but it is hypocritical to make confessions, be forgiven, commit the same sins and then be forgiven again. It seems far too easy to keep admitting to a particular sin, but I suppose it is really a matter for the individual conscience.

Why go through a priest to God? Would it not be possible to sit down and make your own peace with God? Then when you say 'I'm genuinely sorry' it might seem more sincere. Personally, I find many mysterious aspects that do not quite fit, like a jigsaw with a few pieces missing. The same could be said about most religions, and though I have some misgivings about my faith I still believe it is the best. My general criticism of many Catholics is that when I used to go to church I could always tell which ones were there for genuine prayer among the majority, who were looking around to see what other people were wearing. There would be a few nudges if someone arrived who had not attended for a while. This type of thing seemed quite false.

I used the phrase 'when I used to go to church' because although I still go to Mass occasionally, I am no longer a practising Catholic. As a person in the public eye I get a lot of perks and I accept them. If a shopkeeper wants to knock money off some goods to do me a favour I let him, because he wants to do it. I do not like something for nothing, but at the same time I do not insult generosity. If I go to a restaurant I tend to be recognized and asked for autographs, and I accept this and enjoy it, up to a point.

But when I went to church in Liverpool people still made a fuss of me. They wanted to let me know that they knew who I was. They wanted to talk and pestered me to death, thereby defeating the whole object of my going. I felt self-conscious and tense. I had gone to church to relax with my thoughts, but the commotion made me feel the worse for going. I could not get any nearer to God, so what was the point of going? I asked a priest what he suggested. 'Go in the week,' was his reply. 'You don't have to go on Sunday. You're a bit of a special case and if you're going there for prayer, how can you concentrate when everyone's coming up for autographs all the time?'

I took his point, but concluded that perhaps it would be better for me and for everyone else if I did not go to church regularly. I turn to God when I need Him; I am a bit guilty of using Him. I think the main thing is to be Christian in your mind and attempt to be a Christian in your life. I genuinely have time for people and do not believe in drawing any lines.

I argued for an hour with a Jehovah's Witness who wanted to convert me into a follower like Peter Knowles, who used to play for Wolverhampton Wanderers and gave up his career to work for his new faith. Our discussion kept returning to the same point, that I did not have much time for the faith because of their refusal to allow blood transfusions. They are not easily put off and came back to try to get through to my wife, Jean. She is very polite and does not like being nasty to people, but they were getting her down. I had listened to them and put over my point of view, while Jean had done the same. Eventually I told them that I did not want them at the house again.

People used to shy away from religious debate, but television has done much to change that and, though fewer people are going to church, I think church leaders realize that they can still have a religious influence upon people. I have not come across any instances of religious discrimination in football. Even the Protestants of Glasgow Rangers have taken steps to ease their relationship with the Catholics of Celtic by lifting the ban on signing Catholic players. At school religion was mainly an excuse for boys in different coloured uniforms to have a go at each other. I can remember occasional stone-throwing fights against the local 'Proddies' and our football games were always needle matches.

When I was ten our little gang split up into different parts of town. Dave's family moved to Cantley, Maurice's family moved into flats five hundred yards from Spring Gardens and we went to a council house at Waverley Avenue, Balby, two-and-a-quarter miles away. I was sad to leave my friends until I discovered what was waiting for me at Waverley Avenue – a great grassy godsend they called 'the bullring', which was a wonderful sight for a boy who had lived a mile-and-a-half from the nearest park. The bullring was the size of Anfield. One half was made into a little park, the other half was a playing field and a path ran through the middle. It was perfect – ten months of football and two months of cricket, and only the odd complaint from neighbours when a solid cricket ball hit their wall.

Dad had a win on the horses and took me for my first pair of football boots. We went to a sports' shop run by Ray Harrison, who used to play for Doncaster Rovers. A good pair of second-hand boots could be bought for thirty shillings or two pounds. I searched through all the boxes of boots, but every pair I liked was the wrong size, until I found a pair which were fairly pliable and had low heels.

Our matches on the bullring were the type people say would bring the fans flocking back to the grounds – scores of 30–10 and no set pattern of play. We would line up as eleven against eleven, or as many as had turned up, and if a kid could kick the ball a long way he would be a full back while if he was good in the air he would play at centre half, and so on. Oddly enough, if he was not particularly good at anything, we would send him out to one of the wings, where he could do least damage. Coats were put down for goal-posts, causing a multitude of arguments about whether the ball had hit the 'post', scraped inside or gone wide, especially if someone had left a sleeve hanging free from the bundle. The main thing was that we were playing football, sometimes against teams of youngsters from other streets, and learning new skills and tricks. I recall the first time I tried to knock the ball to one side of a player and run round the other side to meet it. I did this against a lad called Barry Watson, who was big and very slow because of his build. Barry was ideal for practising new moves, because it was possible to get away with anything.

We Keegans reacted like television's 'Beverley Hillbillies' when we saw Waverley Avenue. The house was built around the 1930s, had very little character to it and there was no back garden, but it was a palace compared with our previous place. There were three bedrooms, necessary because Mary was reaching the age when a girl needed a room of her own. We took the bath tub but found that there was already one installed. There was also an indoor toilet!

The council, in its wisdom, had brought together families with young children. Older people, like Old Gibby, had gone elsewhere for peace and quiet. There was no main road, no hectic traffic and no tracklesses to run under. There were, however, a great number of boys, inevitably leading to many fights, and I was in the thick of them, small though I was. The build-up to a challenge was traditional. 'He's the cock of the bullring,' the self-styled matchmaker would say, pointing to the boy who was considered to be the boss, the best fighter. 'And you're the new boy,' the boss would say, 'so you are number six.' He would then turn to another boy and proclaim, 'And he's number five.' Once this had been established, number five was honour bound to ask number six, 'Do you want a scrap?' And the fight would begin.

This ritual to show supremacy invariably happens to kids when they move into new areas, and I quickly learned how to take care of myself. I fancied myself as a boxer and begged my father to take me to a club. After a good deal of persuasion he took me to a place called Enfield House, but they had given up boxing, so we became really ambitious and went to the Plant Works Club, which boasted all the local amateur champions, including fully grown men. The club had just started a section for boys of ten or eleven, but it did not last long because there were only three of us of this age and we really knocked each other about. When boxing another boy, we were only the height of the second rope, but still finished with bloody noses. The fellow who ran the club said, 'Come back when you are older.' He was obviously scared of what we might do to each other. I did not go looking for trouble at school, but by the time I was fourteen or fifteen I was rated the second-best fighter in my class. The best fighter was a big fellow, who I did not intend to take on.

Waverley School was just round the corner from our house, which was ideal for my new friends, but, being a Catholic, I was sent to St Francis Xavier School at Balby Bridge, close to the flats where Maurice lived.

St Xavier's was a cosy little school, and when I arrived I was put into Class Four, housed in a little hut, with a fire and a chimney, set apart from the main building but linked by a passageway. Later, when I was running along that passageway, another child, smaller than myself, suddenly appeared in my path and I dived over him to prevent myself knocking him down. Even now I run with my tongue out, and on that occasion I landed with my chin on the concrete and my teeth bit through my tongue, almost severing it. Luckily, I had a tooth missing, otherwise I might have lost my tongue completely. Mrs Gray, one of the teachers, took me to hospital and I held most of my tongue in a handkerchief, clasped to my mouth, until the doctors were able to sew it back on again. I lived on milkshakes for a week.

Sister Mary Oliver was the Headmistress and there were two other nuns at the school. At first some of the kids were a little scared of them, perhaps because of their uniforms. Children tend to be wary of people in uniforms, who represent authority. They gradually grow out of this fear when they go to senior schools. The nuns were good teachers and very versatile. We did not have a sports' master, although Mr McGuinness, a part-time caretaker, would sometimes help out, but frequently one of the nuns would supervise our games. This was how Sister Mary came to spot my talent at football and make a special mention of it in my school report. She was like an angel to us, interested in everything we did and always quick to encourage us.

I was beginning my final year at junior school when Sister Mary wrote about my football, but in my last report from St Xavier's, my form mistress, Mrs Cecilia Wrennall, wrote, 'Kevin has done good work during the year, but his tests were disappointing. He is an exhibitionist, and will do much better when he loses this trait.' These remarks did not go down well at home. Mum and Dad had reason to be proud of my school work because I had been top of the class for every year until then, when I finished second to a girl called Margaret Godfrey. We had a crush on each other, the way kids at school do. As my work faded slightly that year, my friendship with Margaret came on strong.

Margaret did not beat me by much and there were some thirty other children below me, but Dad thought second was a failure after always being first. What annoyed him most was my being described as an exhibitionist. He thought I was giving the nuns trouble and being cheeky, but I always got my laughs in a pleasant way. I was, however, becoming the class idiot, more intent on fooling around and cracking jokes than doing my work. I would chalk on the blackboard, shoot pellets from elastic bands and get up to all kinds of mischief. Mrs Wrennall was right. I was an exhibitionist, although I tried to tell Dad that she was wrong and that I could not understand why she had written such a thing, but he still gave me a good hiding.

By this time I was football daft and a strong supporter of Doncaster Rovers Since I was now travelling to school on the bus, Mum had no objections to my going to the matches at Rovers' ground, Belle Vue, across the road from the racecourse. What she did not know was that I never paid to get in. Mum would give me the money, which I spent on sweets or chips. Two or three of us would go to the match, but we made a detour across a landing strip for light aircraft and climbed over a fence at the back of the ground, with the help of a few spare bricks on which we used to stand. Someone even took the trouble to dig a hole near the fence and we squeezed through that way a few times. There was a joke at Belle Vue that the spectators were climbing out and the police were forcing them to go back in to watch the game, but this was never true in our case. I am not proud to admit that I used to sneak in without paying but that is the sort of thing youngsters get up to.

Being a fanatic, I used to collect footballers' autographs, and one day, when everyone else had gone home after a match, I stood in pouring rain waiting for the players. Eventually, one of my favourites came out – I will not reveal his name because I do not think it would be fair – and I asked him if he would sign his autograph for me. 'Sorry, I haven't got time,' he said. There was no one else around, and he could have quickly scribbled his name and sent me home as the happiest kid in the world. I did not cry, but what he said broke my heart. It also taught me a lesson I have never forgotten. I did not hold it against the player and continued to support him, but if I ever hurt a child like that I would be really upset. I always make time to sign autographs, no matter how much of a hurry I might be in, because I know what it feels like when someone says they do not have the time. I remember that incident more than anything else that happened to me when I was a kid.

One player I shall never forget is Alick Jeffrey. I wish I had seen him in his early days at Doncaster when he was regarded as the best young player in the country. When I watched him he was making a come-back after terrible injury setbacks and had put on extra weight, but he still looked a great player. Sir Alf Ramsey later talked about Martin Peters being ten years ahead of his time, but Jeffrey was ten years ahead of everyone else on the pitch at a time when he was supposedly finished. He had a great shot to go with his other skills. It is easy for people to say that Alick was too fond

FAR LEFT Sporting type, age 4.

LEFT The classroom Mike Yarwood.

Revisiting Sister Mary Oliver at St Xavier's.

of a drink, but if I had experienced what he had gone through, suffering two broken legs just when everything appeared to be developing for him, I think drink would have been a temptation to me.

Another of my Doncaster heroes was Willie Nimmo, a small fellow like myself. We had something else in common, for we both played in goal. That was my position in those days. I was small but agile, and even when I went to Liverpool I still loved to take a turn at diving about the goal during training at Melwood.

Five players from St Xavier's merged with six players from St Peter's to form a team, because both schools were small, and I was the goalkeeper. We played at Town Fields, in Doncaster, where there are about fifteen football pitches. I went by bus wearing my goalkeeper's jersey, shorts and socks, a pair of shoes and carrying my boots. I wore an overcoat and no one could tell I was dressed for football. That worked well in fine weather, but one day it poured with rain and there was mud and puddles all over the pitch. I spent most of the game diving into the mud. Afterwards, the teacher asked me where my clothes were to change into. 'These are them,' I said, indicating my muddy football gear; 'I always come in these.' He did his best to mop me clean, for there were no showers, but I was still filthy when I put on my overcoat and went home again on the bus. Mum had a few choice remarks for me when I walked into the house, 'sludged up to the eyeballs', as she said at the time.

Even though I lost my place at the top of the class, I managed to pass my eleven-plus examination. This did not come as a surprise, because I had been placed first three times and then second in my final year at junior school, and I was especially strong at mental arithmetic. I was still relieved to get the results, because, no matter how clever one is, there is always the possibility of an off day when the exams come round. I moved to another school called St Peter's, six miles away at Cantley, where David Anderson then lived. St Peter's was a secondary school with a grammar department for those with scholarships. The uniforms were the same for pupils in both departments, except that the grammar boys had blue braiding round the cuffs and pockets. This sign of segregation caused some aggravation among the boys.

At junior school I had played around but still done the work, and this set the wrong pattern for the rest of my school life. As the work became more intense, so my clowning became more pronounced. I used to mimic people and was never short of an audience. It was not long before my work deteriorated. Though I was good at working out figures in my head, I just could not fathom geometry and algebra. I could see nothing to be gained by working out angles and talking about buying two x pounds of potatoes. I now realize how foolish I was.

When we were given homework, I used to copy it from other boys the following morning, but I knew the teachers were not taken in. Mr Murphy, my form master, and Mr Gormley, the housemaster and sports master, had taught at Borstal and were both very strong on discipline. I often got the stick, most times quite deservedly. Once, I even tried the old trick from the schoolboy comics of putting a book down the seat of my pants, but this only earned me twelve strokes instead of six and Mr Murphy used the cane on my hands instead of my backside. Our Latin master was an Asian, who usually enjoyed a joke. During one of his lessons I tried to be amusing, but he

Progress at St Peter's . . . ABOVE The intermediate (second right, front row) . . . and BELOW
The senior (third right, front row).

took exception to me. He dragged me to the front of the class and rapped my knuckles so hard with the back of a blackboard eraser that they became swollen.

I envied the boys who could do woodwork, because I gave it up as a bad job after a year. When we finished making whatever we had chosen or been set to do, we would line up to have our work marked out of ten by the master, Mr Ackroyd. I made a foot-stool – that was what it was supposed to be – but the joints fitted so badly that I filled the gaps with wood shavings and glue. A boy called John Brown, who was ahead of me in the queue, had made a towel rack, with joints no better than mine. John, however, had not bothered to 'improve' them and when Mr Ackroyd saw his rack, he cracked him over the head with it. That made me laugh, and I was still laughing when I handed my work to the master. He took one look at it, saw how I had cheated by filling up the joints, and just tapped me gently on the head with the stool. The legs fell to the floor and Mr Ackroyd was left holding the wicker top. At the end of the year I decided to change subjects and tried art instead. After football, I enjoyed art lessons more than anything else at school – I loved splashing around with the paint.

When I meet old school friends they often say I fooled around at school because I knew I was going to end up playing football for a living. That is not true. I had no idea I would become a footballer. I was not thinking about the future, even though my antics were obviously putting my future at risk. I was simply enjoying myself.

3

Trials...and tribulations

It came as a shock when I was told that my career as a goalkeeper was over. Mr Teanby, the history teacher who also looked after the intermediate (first and second years) football team at St Peter's, was the man who took that decision. 'If you want to play for this team you will have to play out, because you are not big enough to be in goal,' he said, and put me on the wing. I played on one wing and a boy called Kevin Scott played on the other. We were both midgets. I had been happy being a goalkeeper. Though I had often played outfield in kick-about games, all my serious practice had been in goal. I was now being denied the position because of my height, which was less than five feet.

At first, I did not take too kindly to the idea, but I can smile when I look back. Several small players have become good goalkeepers. I idolized Willie Nimmo at Doncaster, and there was Eddie Hopkinson at Bolton Wanderers and Alan Hodgkinson at Sheffield United. More recently, Derby County had a little goalkeeper called Les Green. Most clubs, especially Liverpool, believe goalkeepers are born, not made; born with the build and born for the job. When taking on an apprentice, they watched how he developed physically. They were often more concerned with his build than his ability.

Dad often said that, 'a good big 'un will always beat a good little 'un.' Although I argued that it was not always true, when studying top-class sport, size does count in most cases. Basketball in America is the best example. You might be a very good player, but if you are only five foot ten inches or even six foot you would have a job making the major league in America, where they go for seven footers.

In football, a large goalkeeper will always be the one in most demand, but I tried to prove to Dad that when it comes to outfield players 'a good little 'un can beat a good big 'un'. I believe I am lucky to be small, because it eventually helped me to get noticed. If I had been a big fellow, the tricks I was doing might not have appeared as impressive as they did. Spectators always like to see a small man leap up at the far post to head a great goal. A big striker doing the same thing is nothing out of the ordinary as far as they are concerned.

There were times as a youngster when people made my height a handicap, but as things turned out, Mr Teanby did me a favour. He replaced me in goal with a lad from the second year called Arthur Cadman. Arthur was five feet ten inches and skinny, but even though he took my position, we became good friends. There was only one other boy, apart from Arthur, from the second year in the team, which was allowed to mature. It was a little similar to playing a lot of apprentices in a First Division team.

After a few hammerings, we would eventually benefit from the experience. By our second season we were a good side, winning the local intermediate league and cup. By the time we had progressed through to the fourth year, as seniors, we swept all before us. Three players scored 130 goals between themselves, about forty of which were mine.

The chance of a trial with Doncaster Rovers should have been one of the highlights of my life, but there was some confusion and it became an anti-climax. I was fourteen and still at school when someone made an arrangement with my father for me to go to Belle Vue and play in a trial match. I was told to report at the ground for 6.30 on a particular evening. I gathered my playing kit, my boots and a towel, and set off on the bus, but when I arrived the ground was deserted. The trialists had gone off to where they were playing the match, and I could only go back home again. Apparently, the other boys had been told to turn up at six o'clock. I told my father he had got the times wrong, but he insisted that he had been told 6.30. The whole business is still somewhat confusing, but I felt that some of the men who drank with Dad at the pub pretended they knew something that they didn't, and that Rovers did not want me at all.

I decided to take the hint. I was not too pleased that I had gone all the way to the ground for nothing, but perhaps things had worked out for the best. I reasoned that it was better to have turned up at the wrong time than to have played in a trial, only to be told I was not good enough. I was still only a kid, without the confidence I now have. I had skill but no real pace or any great strength in my legs. Neither did I have the build. It was the nearest I ever came to joining my home team, my boyhood idols.

At that time I did not think I would become a professional footballer at all, and what happened at Doncaster was only one of a series of incidents that added conviction to that feeling. Shortly afterwards, I had an opportunity to go for trials at Coventry City as an associated schoolboy, with the possibility of being taken on as an apprentice professional if they thought I was good enough. If I was to have the trial, I would have to break off school before the holidays, necessitating Dad asking for permission. He saw the Headmaster, Mr Smith, who called in Mr Gormley, the sports' master, and asked for his opinion. Mr Gormley told the Headmaster that he had better make me stay at school because, in his opinion, I would never make a footballer as long as I lived.

In spite of that recommendation, I was allowed to go to Coventry. A hundred boys began the trial, the number being whittled down to two who would have six weeks of matches and training. I was one of them. It was such a bonus for me to be training with and playing against the professionals. I remember Ray Pointer running round the track to get fit again after recovering from an injury. Then there was Bill Glazier, the goalkeeper, and George Curtis, a large, impressive fellow, with Willie Carr, only a kid himself but already being talked about as a future Scottish international. I played against a few teams and scored some goals, doing my best to impress the older professionals when we went on a cross-country run. 'Hey, you young bugger, slow down!' they shouted. I can imagine the same thing happening if a youngster did that at Liverpool.

Dad had arranged for me to stay with Uncle Frank, who was living at Stockingford, near Nuneaton, and to help pay my board, my uncle got me a job with a friend of his spraying cars. My job was to put Polyfilla on the damaged bodywork and rub it down until the surface was smooth and ready for spraying. He would leave me for hours and then take a look at what I had done. By the time I had finished rubbing, I would be back to the metal again, and he would finish up having to do the job himself. 'Do something useful – sweep up!' he would say. The job lasted for five weeks, until eventually he told me I would have to go because I was not good enough.

At the end of the trial period, Coventry's youth team manager, Graham Hill, told me that 'we think you have the ability, but we don't think you have the height or the build.' I took that as a nice way of saying they did not think I was good enough, although in fairness I was still only five foot tall. Some two years later I had shot up to five foot six inches, and now my height is five foot seven inches.

The other boy, who was kept on, was Brian Joy. We were about equal as far as ability was concerned, but he had the better build, being much taller than me, and looking far more the part. Brian's career has since taken him to Doncaster, Torquay, Tranmere and Exeter. He has had a succession of bad injuries, making things pretty rough for him.

Jimmy Hill was the Coventry manager at the time of my trial. He knows his club turned me down because I always tried to make a point of scoring a goal when I played against Coventry. Not that it was Jimmy Hill's job to sort out the young trialists, but I held it against him at the time!

I suppose Dad was disappointed, but he never said anything about it. He was always very good that way, never seeing anything wrong with me. Even when I had had a poor game he would still say that I was 'the best player on the park'. But what Mr Gormley had said still rankled with me. I felt it was a little harsh because I was one of the best players at school. I thought he would have encouraged me because I enjoyed playing for him. It did not, however, make me lose faith in myself. When people have believed in me and given me responsibility I have been a better player for it. But when people have done me down, I have managed to fight back and still come through. Mr Gormley was entitled to his opinion. I saw him again not long ago at a garden fête, when he tried to give me the impression that he had known all along that I would make it. Deep down, I am sure he will admit he said otherwise. I think I surprised a few people because I was a late developer.

When I was fifteen I went to trials for Doncaster Boys and most of the kids at school said that I was sure to be successful. In fact, two other lads from St Peter's got in and I was left out. The boy who kept me out was Kevin Johnson, from Bentley West End School. Kevin was as small as me, a year younger and a better player. He had an extremely good left foot. When I thought of him I became a little disheartened, because if I was seriously thinking of making it, he had to be a superstar. Sure enough, Kevin was signed by Sheffield Wednesday and everyone thought he would be a great player. But things did not work out for him. He was given a free transfer to Workington and later moved to Hartlepool United and then Huddersfield Town.

I was waiting to play in a First Division game for Liverpool at Newcastle United, when a lad a little smaller than me came up and said, 'Do you remember me?' It was Kevin.

'Yes, I do,' I said. 'How are you? Who are you playing for?'

'Hartlepools,' he replied.

'Not so good,' I said, and he told me he did not like it there much. He asked me if I could get him a ticket, which I was able to do.

Our meeting typified football for me; the way his life had turned for the worse while mine had turned for the better. It illustrated how difficult it is to assess a footballer when he is so young. There are many obstacles for aspiring footballers from the age of fifteen to eighteen. You can be the best player in the world, but might not like living in digs, or become too fond of diversions such as drinking, smoking and women. I am not saying Kevin Johnson fell foul of these diversions. I do not know his story, but somewhere along the line, whether it was Sheffield Wednesday's fault or his own, a great young player went astray. It might have been his attitude. He might not have had the nerve. He might not have been strong enough. He might not have had the heart for it. It could have been so many things.

When you get to First Division level, you can have a high degree of skill but something might still be missing. If you are not totally dedicated, you will not make it. The same applies if you have no pace or no courage – a 'bottler' as they say in the game. If you are unlucky enough to be injury prone you will also not make it. Sometimes it is hard to put your finger on the reason for a player's failure. Perhaps, Kevin was just an early developer. I am always sceptical when people talk about 'the best young player I've seen in my life'. He might be, but often the worst thing that could happen for the player is to have the fact continually rammed down his throat. How will he react to it? Will it make him even better or will it go to his head and ruin him?

Kevin Johnson might yet make a higher grade than the Fourth Division, if he still has the talent that impressed everyone so much when he was a schoolboy. I hope he does. I was fortunate in being able to gauge things more gradually. Instead of being rushed off to a big club I had to think first about getting a job. I started at the bottom instead of near the top or even half-way up the ladder. I continue to maintain that without a little slice of luck I would still be playing local football in Doncaster. I did not let my early setbacks get me down. I was too busy getting involved in all kinds of sporting activities to have time to mope.

I was captain of St Peter's cricket team. This kept me occupied during the period when the goal-posts were down, but we were not brilliant by any standards. Most of the grammar schools, and ours was only the grammar department of a secondary school, had good cricket teams because they placed a great deal of emphasis on the game. We were less fanatical about it, and it showed in our performances. For instance, I put one grammar school in to bat and they scored some two hundred runs for three wickets and we were all out for twelve. I played a real captain's part, being out for a duck, first ball, while our star batsman scored only eight. But we did manage to win a couple of matches.

Then there was running. I was the school mile champion and came fifth in the Doncaster schools' cross-country championships. I never rated myself as a sprinter. I am as quick with a ball as without one, but am not a flyer by any means.

At this time I began to play football for Enfield House Youth Club, in the centre of Doncaster. The club was rough by reputation and every time I went there was a boy standing outside holding a huge knife, which he would throw into the wooden gate. The story went round that he had been banned two years earlier and was waiting for the warden to come out so that he could get his revenge. That was typical of the way children exaggerate, but he was outside the club every night for two years and he used to scare me stiff. If Mum had known about him she would not have let me go.

Rough or not, Enfield House was the ideal place for me. There were pop record sessions, appearances by local pop groups, table tennis and, most important of all, a gymnasium in which I could train for two nights a week. At Enfield House I began to take the first measures towards building my physique through weight training, but it did not last long. What put me off was the sight of a massive lad called Mick Hughes, who used to train with the weights most of the time. I did not want to look like him, and I left the weights alone. I later realized that Mick was the type who took training to extremes, and I returned to the weights again. It was not until I went to Scunthorpe United that I seriously began to develop my body with weights. One of the players, Derek Hemstead, who went on to Carlisle United, was a fitness fanatic, and I tried to follow the example he set. One of his favourite exercises was to run up and down the grandstand steps at Scunthorpe, and his calf muscles were bigger than my thigh muscles.

Part of our training at the youth club was a run of four or five miles, across Hyde Park and round the racecourse. When we became quite proficient at this, we decided to offer to make a run for charity. We contacted a man who organized holidays for local orphans, and he arranged for seven of us, including two girls, to be sponsored. The distance was fifty miles, from Manchester to Doncaster. Whoever chose the route must have been a sadist! First, we travelled to Manchester by car covering the course we would use – hills all the way – the mere sight of which made us feel exhausted before we had even started.

We set off from Piccadilly station, trailed by cars full of rescuers carrying soup, biscuits, energy tablets and first-aid kits. We thought we had trained hard for the run, covering between fifteen and twenty miles around Doncaster some nights, but we had no idea what it would really be like. Place names became milestones in our minds. Woodhead . . . Penistone . . . Barnsley . . . Doncaster – each one seemed beyond our reach. After fourteen miles the girls dropped out. They had done well. The first of the boys to flag was at sixteen miles. Another left at eighteen miles and the next followed at twenty-one miles. That left me and a friend, Dave Brown. All that kept going through our minds was, 'How the hell are we going to get to Doncaster?' A civic reception had been arranged there for 3.00 pm, but at one o'clock we were only on the outskirts of Penistone, four-and-a-half miles from Barnsley.

Our legs were just about to take the strain of a steep hill when I asked Dave, 'How are you feeling?'

'Fine,' he replied. 'I think we are going to do it.'

'Yes, we are,' I assured him.

We kept on climbing, somehow willing our legs to match our spirits, but the cars which passed us by made us feel that we were moving backwards.

'I'm fine,' repeated Dave.

Less than a minute later I heard a thump and turned to see Dave flat on the ground where he had collapsed, striking his head on the concrete. He was out cold, after thirty-one miles. I continued to jog on the spot until one of the back-up cars reached us, and I felt ill suddenly just thinking about Dave's fall. I helped to drag him into the car, making sure I did not stop the jogging. He looked completely exhausted, almost as if he was dead. His feet were sticking out of the back door of the car as the occupants tried to bring him round. Eventually I managed to say something: 'I'd better keep on going, hadn't I?'

'Yes,' they said, 'you've got to finish.' The people in the car then did the worst thing they could possibly have done. They sent out the boy who had stopped after sixteen miles to keep me company, but by then he had recovered and was almost as fresh as a daisy. He made me feel even worse. Seeing how fresh he was made me realize how tired I was. I struggled on over the hills until I was about a mile-and-a-half from the centre of Barnsley. Then my legs buckled. I did not fall, but had stopped running and was swaying all over the road. I had lost my sense of balance and was finished.

We were disappointed, but, having been sponsored for each mile, we still made a few bob for the children. I have often driven that way since, and never pass the spot where Dave collapsed without smiling to myself and feeling thankful I am in the car.

Showing the resilience of youth, we decided to try another fifty-mile run, but this time using a more sensible, less hazardous route from Nottingham to Doncaster. Billy Gray, then the manager of Notts County, started us off. On this occasion three of us – Dave, Alan Dykes and myself – managed to complete the course. We set a fair pace from the start, some of the other boys being annoyed that we went off so quickly, but we had learnt from the bitter experience of the first run that the only way we were going to succeed was to keep to a faster time schedule. There is a limit to how long one can keep on running, and we realized we had gone too slowly the first time.

The run began at approximately 7.30 in the morning. I can still remember some of the odd, detached thoughts that went through my mind as a I jogged along. It is strange how your mind can wander away and lose itself when you are running. If you only thought about the running I am sure you would soon pack it in as a crazy idea. I recall running past some posh houses somewhere along the route, and a man reversing an expensive sports-car out of his drive. Even when I had run further on, that fellow and his sports-car were still dominating my thoughts. I wondered what his job was, whether he had earned his money or married into it. I respect people who work hard and become successful while I tend to be prejudiced against those who marry into money. I do not know why really; I just think it must be awful to become rich that way, although many people consider it the greatest stroke of good fortune imaginable.

I also had random thoughts about my family. I remembered people from long ago in my childhood and wondered what they were doing, wishing I had kept in touch with them. Nagging little problems would surface, which I would try to work out. My mind and body were functioning quite separately. When I went over those thoughts later, none of them seemed to make much sense.

As we approached Doncaster in triumph, a police escort led us into town, past the

Rovers' ground and the racecourse. Everyone was delighted for us and we were even given a civic reception at the mayor's parlour. I looked at Dave and remembered the mornings I had seen him jogging out of his house at seven o'clock. What an amazing lad – a fitness fanatic one minute, and smoking and drinking the next! That run was possibly the greatest achievement of Dave's life. It was definitely one of my greatest achievements.

When England won the World Cup in 1966 I was fifteen and in my fourth year at St Peter's. I played that series, kick for kick, with my mates in the bullring. 'We'll be England – you be Argentina,' we would say, reliving the matches we had seen on television. At the start people talked about Brazil, Argentina and Italy, but as the competition built up we began to realize that England had a chance of winning. I could not wait for the Final against West Germany to start. I was in a high state of excitement from the moment I opened my eyes that Saturday morning, and was so proud when England won.

As a schoolboy, I saw Bobby Moore pick up the World Cup. Yet seven years later he was my captain, leading me out for England against Wales in a World Cup qualifying match. I played against most of the players who won the World Cup – Gordon Banks, Bobby Moore, the Charlton brothers, Geoff Hurst and Alan Ball. Ballie really caught my imagination in 1966. There he was, a little fellow like myself, making an enormous impact on the game. Banks played against Liverpool at Anfield on the Saturday before the car crash in which he injured his eye. That match was, sadly, his last in top-class football.

A month before the GCE 'O' Level examinations at St Peter's, the history master, Mr McManus, who tended to humour me during my bouts of foolery, told me straight: 'You've messed about so much that I'm not going to put you in for the exam because it would be pointless.' That really annoyed me. When people belittle me in this way I see it as a challenge and do my best to rise to it and prove them wrong, 'I'll show him!' I thought. 'Put me in for that exam, because I want to take it,' I told Mr McManus. Although he said I did not deserve it, he eventually agreed to enter me.

Although I took seven subjects, history was the only one I studied hard during the weeks leading up to the exams. I worked at it, parrot fashion, determined to do well in this subject. Mr McManus told me what sort of questions to expect, but he was the most surprised teacher in the world when I passed. 'I don't know how you did it!' he said. The only other subject I passed was art, the switch from woodwork not being in vain. Mr Lloyd, the master, told four of us in his class, 'We have no Leonardo da Vincis here, but there's always the landscape, and if you get a good average mark for your landscape you should pass.' Whenever we had art I would paint landscapes for two hours. I worked at it until I could paint the same scene without too much difficulty. In the exam we were also asked to paint a bowl of fruit in still life – I was always able to paint reasonably well when it was simply a matter of copying a subject.

Having stayed at school until the fifth form to gain some qualifications, and armed with my 'O' Levels in history and art, it was then time for me to find a job.

4

Peglers Brass Works reserves

The recruiting and training officer at Peglers Brass Works in Doncaster was thorough and to the point.

'You went to St Peter's?'

'Yes.'

'And now you are sixteen?'

'Fifteen, going on sixteen.'

'You've got some qualifications, have you?'

'Yes, I've got two 'O' Levels.'

'Very good. Of course, you don't need them for this job.'

'No, I realize that.'

'And what makes you want to do it?'

'I fancy it.'

'What are your 'O' Levels?'

'Art and history.'

'They're not much good to you. If you had got history and maths, then you would be talking.'

I thought that was rich considering I had put in an extra year at school and was feeling quite chuffed with my art and history. Though I didn't need a degree to become a clerk at Peglers, I was given an aptitude test by the recruiting and training officer. One of the requirements was to write a description of a post-box. At first, this seemed stupid but, after a little more thought, I realized there are many different kinds of post-boxes. They come in various shapes and sizes. Some stand alone and are independent, while others are built on to a post office building or a countryside wall. They have the monarch's initials, plates inscribed with collection times, special locks, and so on. I passed the test and got the job, though I could not help feeling I was the only one who had applied for it.

When I left school, in 1966, it was not too difficult for reasonably intelligent children to find jobs, even without a string of qualifications that stretched the length of an arm. It is very different for youngsters today. No wonder some of them drop out of society, when society can find so little to offer in the way of employment. I never had any thoughts about going to university, but if I had gone and got a degree there would have been no worries about finally getting a suitable job. Most university graduates are now not nearly as fortunate.

Peglers make a whole of range of products, including taps and toilet fittings, and

I became a clerk in their central stores. I was a middleman between the brass foundry and the production line. Parts would be sent up from the foundry – cotterpins, ballcock valves and so on – and I had to keep a check to make sure there was enough stock of each to continue work on a particular line. Otherwise, the girls in the factory would switch to assembling another line, such as hot and cold mixer-taps.

At first, I thought it was a marvellous job, because I was surrounded by girls, but soon they almost scared the pants off me. Factory girls are worse than men when they get together, and after they saw how young I was they began to tease me. 'Wait until Christmas,' they kept saying. I asked the men in the store what they meant and was told that, 'At Christmas they'll get you, strip you and grease you all over!'

After that I led the life of a fugitive. Mr Leatherland, the head of the stores, would ask me to deliver letters to other departments, no more than two hundred yards away by the most direct route through the factory, but I was so afraid of what those girls might do to me that I would take the longer way round to avoid them. This would take me ages, and I am sure Mr Leatherland thought I was skiving. Fortunately, I missed the threatened Christmas initiation ceremony. Having started work in July, I left at the end of the following September to begin life as a professional footballer, grateful to Peglers for having put up with me in their reserve team.

Our working area in central stores was cramped. There were four desks and five of us – Alf, who was teaching me the job, Lennie, Les, Harry and me. Peglers had two football teams, Harry being the manager of the reserves. When he asked me if I played football, I said I liked the game and had played for my school and the youth club. I did not mention that I had been to Coventry for a trial because I did not want them to think I was bragging. Harry offered to give me a game. They were a good set of lads. The first team played in the local senior league and we played in the Bentley League. I enjoyed every minute of it. Our home pitch was at Peglers' sports ground, which has been levelled now, but when I played there was a big kink in the middle. If you kicked the ball hard it would hit the rise of the ground and bounce back at you. If you looked from the other end at players running towards you, first you would see heads and bodies and then suddenly legs would appear.

We were serious about our matches, but they were also great fun because we were a good bunch of lads and not all of us could play. Lennie, our goalkeeper, was a big fellow who could crunch a few of the opposing forwards, but let the odd shot slip under his body. All week Harry and I would say to him, 'Haven't you had a letter from the Nabisco people yet, Lennie?' We were pulling his leg about a Weetabix advertisement on the television, which featured a harassed goalkeeper. We also joked that when Lennie let in a lot of goals and the manager told him off, he would put his head in his hands ... and drop it! He took it all very well and kept saying he was going to retire, but his career was filled with comebacks.

I played a couple of times for Peglers' first team when one of their regulars was injured but I knew the player would get his place back when he was fit again and I did not really enjoy those games. The first team was quite successful but the players took the game a little too seriously. That is probably why they did not think I was good enough for them. It seemed to be their whole lives, whereas to me it was just good fun, although their attitude gave me an insight into what professional football would be like. The higher up the scale you go in the game, the less you enjoy football. I have always prided myself that although I might be in a game that has many pressures, I can still have a laugh occasionally on the field.

Peglers' reserve team was not successful, just a middle of the table side, and, although we did not like to lose, we played our football with a smile. Our shirts were tatty with massive stripes, and mine was so big that the number ten – I played in midfield – spread half-way round my body.

Harry was no youngster, but he had been around in local football and could still play a bit. He was always hoping one of us would not turn up, so he could get a game. When this happened, Harry's fitness did not match his enthusiasm. He was short of pace, losing his touch and occasionally would fall over the ball. We would tease him all week when that happened.

On our ground, you might receive a pass, beat an opponent with a dribble and start running uphill with the ball, but if you had not judged the change of ground level you would be running uphill while the ball was running downhill. That pitch was not good, especially for old men like Harry!

At this time I was playing three times a week, giving me a treble chance of being spotted by a professional club. I played for Peglers' reserves on Saturday morning, for Enfield House Youth Club on Saturday afternoon and for the Lonsdale Hotel in the Sunday League the following afternoon – without ever going into the pub! All this was good experience, and my first break came as a result of playing for Lonsdale, not far from the racecourse. The Sunday League was made up of a premier and three other divisions. When I joined them, Lonsdale were in the second division. Dad got me fixed up with the team through a friend of his. Lonsdale were good, though not quite as good as the Peglers' first team, and we won promotion to the first division.

Bob Nellis, who became chairman of Doncaster Rugby League Club, played Sunday League soccer for one of our rivals, Woodfield Social. He also supervised a team of youngsters on Saturday mornings, and on one such occasion Jeff Barker, the chief scout of Scunthorpe United, approached him. 'If you ever get any good young lads who you think are League standard or good enough to be apprentices or deserve a trial, Scunthorpe will have a look at them,' said Jeff. The following day, Bob, who would be about twenty-four, was marking me in a game between Woodfield and Lonsdale. A former trialist with Doncaster Rovers, he was a little chubby but could still play, although I have joked with him that he was so bad that he made me look good. After that match he told me about Scunthorpe United, and asked if I was interested. I said yes.

Scunthorpe agreed to give me a series of trials with their intermediate team on Saturday mornings. Bob was a salesman for a furniture and drapery firm called Madorco House, not forty yards from where I had lived at Spring Gardens. Each Saturday morning he would collect me in his car at 8.30 and we would set off in the general direction of Scunthorpe, set to arrive at eleven o'clock. Usually this is only a journey of twenty-four miles, but Bob would call to see some of his customers on the way. We went all over the place, and by the time we arrived at the ground it seemed as if we had driven two hundred miles.

It was kind of Bob to go to so much trouble to help me. After I had played four or five trial games for Scunthorpe, they decided to sign me, though I do not think they were particularly keen about me. Bob has his own shop now. He was always a good salesman, able to talk his way into anything and I am glad he talked me into going to Scunthorpe.

5

The Old Show Ground

The apprentice professional footballers at Scunthorpe United were more like odd job boys. Ron Ashman, the manager, catching us neglecting our work to have a kick around, would say, 'Anybody would think you were here to play football! You are here to scrub out the toilets and clean the bath.' We were also there to climb the steps of the pylons and wash the floodlights and to sweep the terracing of the Old Show Ground. These jobs were laborious and boring, but we found a way to brighten our day. The club had an ancient tractor, with pieces of its bodywork missing and the manufacturer's name long since departed, but the engine was alive and willing. When we had filled the dustbins with the rubbish from the terracing, we would use the tractor to transport them round to the tip at the back of the stand.

One day, after sweeping faster than usual and emptying the dustbins, we decided to build a track round the field leading to the tip. When Jack Brownsword, the club's trainer-coach, saw us at work on the track, he was delighted, thinking that we were building it to speed up the job of clearing away the rubbish. In fact, we were building a course on which to put the tractor through time trials. There were five of us – Nigel (Nige) Jackson, Jimmy Coyne, Steve (Nobby) Hibbotson, Alan Olbison and me – and we 'borrowed' Jack's stop-watch.

Nige set off on the tractor first and was timed at just over thirty-two seconds, which we all thought was quite good. Nobby, a gutsy fellow slightly smaller than me, shot into the lead with a time of 28·6. Jimmy tried to better that and failed miserably, having trouble in negotiating a bend. Then it was my turn. I had watched my rivals closely as they charged around the course, which included a hill. I noticed that the faster the hill was approached, the further the tractor would leap forward before touching down on the other side. Here was a possible tactical advantage. I went for that hill, determined to break all records. Sure enough, the tractor shot into the air, but landed with a great bang, a mighty fizzle, and a great deal of sparks and steam. The impact of the landing had forced the axle up through the engine and the whole front collapsed in a heap of smoking metal.

We tried to lift it up and push it back to the shed, where it was garaged, wondering how we could explain to Jack what had happened. We could not delay this because the tractor was needed in the everyday running of the club. Nige was selected to break the news, because he got on well with Jack by regularly washing his car. The rest of us remained round the side of the stand with the tractor, making forlorn attempts to improve it by knocking the axle out of the engine with a large hammer.

A night out with Scunthorpe. Back row (from left): Jack Brownsword (trainer), Geoff Bernard, Charlie Strong (physiotherapist), Jeff Barker (assistant manager), George Kerr, Nige Cassidy, John Barker, Mick Atkin, Terry Heath, Steve Deere, Ron Ashman (manager). Front: Nige Jackson, me, Barry Lindsay, Don Welbourne, Graham Rusling, Angus Davidson, Graham Foxton.

Final instructions before the run from Manchester (I'm third from the left, leaning on the car).

K.K.—D

We were extremely worried. I was on the fringe of the first team and thought I might just keep my job and escape with a fine, but for a couple of the boys the incident could have meant the difference between being in and out of football. I felt terrible about the whole thing. Eventually Jack arrived with Nige, took one look at the tractor and gave us a right rollicking. Then he said, 'You've got to see the boss.'

Ron Ashman added to Jack's roasting: 'What you have got to learn now is that you are not schoolboys up to pranks. You are in a professional sport. You are some of the lucky ones who have been chosen as apprentices at this club, and you should respect it.'

When we left his office I am sure Ron had a little chuckle about it, but it was not a laughing matter for Scunthorpe to have to repair that tractor. It cost them at least £100 – they must have bought the parts from an antique dealer – which was a lot of money then to a Fourth Division club. We were very apologetic and offered to pay for the damage out of our wages. Fortunately, they did not take us up on that, because I was only earning seven pounds a week, four pounds of which went to pay for my digs.

I was better off than when I worked at Peglers, where my first pay packet was between £4 and £5, which was then average for sixteen-year-olds. With overtime, I could draw £8 at Peglers, but went straight on to £7 basic as an apprentice at Scunthorpe. As I made progress I graduated to £8 a week, then £10, £20 and finished up with £30 a week.

Only once did I quibble about my wages at Scunthorpe. When I was earning a basic £7 plus £2 bonus for playing in the reserves, I was selected for the first team against Arsenal in a League Cup tie at the Old Show Ground. The game was watched by 17,450 spectators, the first teamers picking up more than £100 each while I ended up with £7. I had forfeited my £2 reserve team bonus, which meant the reserve players had made £2 more than me. Dad was especially upset about this. He felt that if the club were not prepared to give me a little extra the other first team players should have had a whip-round to ensure that I shared in their big pay-day. At the time, I was not too worried about it. I was glad to have had the opportunity to have played in a glamour game, but later did feel somewhat cheated. I had played in what was then the biggest game of my life, and had been paid less than anybody else at the club.

Before the Arsenal game I had played only four times in the Fourth Division, and it gave me a tremendous lift. But the match I remember most from my days with Scunthorpe was the one in which we knocked Sheffield Wednesday out of the FA Cup at Hillsborough. In the fourth round we had beaten Millwall, with Keith Weller and Derek Possee in their team, which gave us a chance to have a crack at a First Division team on their own ground – Wednesday were then experiencing happier times than at present. It was a strange type of game, because we never dominated our opponents and they missed some chances after scoring very early in the game. When the ball went into our net we were expecting a score of something like 7–0, but we recovered, Sheffield Wednesday lost their way and we beat then 2–1. I had played better, but I worked hard and did my part. It was wonderful to see how happy we had made our supporters. We were drawn away to Swindon in the next round, but were unfortunately beaten.

The player everyone wanted to talk to during our cup run was Nigel Cassidy, who was later transferred to Oxford United. Nige seemed to attract all the headlines. He was a good player, but there was not a bad set of players around him. Although he was scoring his goals, someone was crossing the ball for him. Nige was to Scunthorpe then what I later became to Liverpool, and I know it used to annoy the other lads when he was getting all the publicity. I suppose some of the Liverpool players have felt a bit choked about the publicity that has come my way. While I admit I enjoyed it at first, because I was young and I thought my day had come, it does work both ways. When you have made a name for yourself in football, you tend to get more attention from the press. Sometimes, I have left the field thinking I have not had a particularly good game, but some reporters have raved about me, overlooking another player who has had a better game. But you also tend to come in for much more criticism. If an average player has a poor game, nothing is said. Half the crowd and the press expect them to have no more than an average match. But people now make a point of it when I have a poor game. I suppose you become a victim of your own standards.

All this is far removed from my beginnings in professional football, when I used to take turns with Nige Jackson at driving the team bus to one of Scunthorpe intermediates' away matches. There were no time trials, of course! We would play clubs such as Newcastle United and get beaten 8–0 – a good result for us considering Newcastle would field of a team of apprentices while we would have only three, the rest of the team being made up of amateurs. We did not train or play together during the week and, as a result, we used to get some drubbings when we were stuck out to play together on Saturdays.

Even so, I loved playing for the intermediates. When I was selected for the first team I asked the manager if I could play for the intermediates on the Saturday following a Friday night match in the League. On one occasion, I had a good game against Chesterfield in the Fourth Division on the Friday night, but could do nothing right for the intermediates when we were beaten by Sheffield Wednesday juniors the following day. Derek Hemstead was the player who showed me what could be achieved by training above and beyond the call of duty, and my work with weights, under professional supervision, developed my body to suit an all-action game.

There were some hard cases around. We had a goalkeeper, Jim Lavery, a Scot, who used to dive full-length on the car park when we were having a practice. The week Ron Ashman gave Jim a free transfer, we were training in the gym at a local leisure centre. The manager joined us in a five-a-side match, and every time he received the ball, Jim would go after him and make a crunching tackle. Eventually, Jim slid full-length, stuck his feet up against a wall and the boss went flying over the outstretched legs, landing on his face. That was no way to treat Ron Ashman, a man who deserved a great deal of respect.

I took to Jack Brownsword from the moment I arrived at the Old Show Ground, and owe him a lot. Jack was born in Doncaster and, like my father, had been a miner. As a player, he had a remarkable career at Scunthorpe, where he was one of the most loyal servants to one club that the game has known. People tell me he was one of the best uncapped full backs in the country. As the club's trainer he helped me enormously, both in a practical sense and also with his sound advice. 'The thing that impresses most people about you is that you are a one hundred per center,' he used to tell me. 'Every time you run, whether it be twice round the rugby pitch, four times round the ground, or on a cross-country, you always want to be first. Never lose that, because it's the biggest thing you've got going for you.'

Jack's idea of a cross-country run was a killer. We went to a big hill on the edge of Scunthorpe called Atkinson's Warren, or 'Ackie's Warren' as we knew it. This was at Flixborough, the village where, in 1974, twenty-eight people were killed and 155 injured in an explosion at the Nypro Chemical Works. From the top of the hill, on a clear day, you could see Doncaster, and I sometimes wished I was there and not at 'Ackie's'. Jack split us into two groups of twelve or thirteen, and we would start from the top of the hill and run down. That might sound easy, but the ground was so steep that it was difficult to keep your balance and stop yourself from moving too fast. If the downward journey was tough, then the trip back up again was even harder. Half-way up was a sand pit, stretching for about thirty yards, and the sand would shift and drain the strength from our legs.

After we had run up and down the hill six times, we would set off round Flixborough. This was a most demanding training session, and, though the benefit from it was enormous in terms of stamina, it used to take its toll, especially on new arrivals at the club. I was told about a coloured lad called Peter Foley, who went on to play in the Northern Premier League. After three assaults on 'Ackie's', Peter lost his balance. He came through the sand and tried to pump his legs to make some headway on the firmer ground. His legs would not respond and he began to sway, eventually collapsing into a bush of thorns. Most new boys used to spew up after a session at 'Ackie's', but this did not happen to me because of my previous experience running for the youth club and the school.

Derek Hemstead and I used to win the cross-country every week, with most of the other players straggling in together. Some used to cheat by taking lifts on cattle trucks, but Jack used to say they were only cheating themselves by doing that. On one occasion, when Derek and I were jogging round the three-mile course after completing the hill climbs, we saw a group of fifteen to twenty other players taking a short cut across ploughed fields. When they met up with us, we were allowed to run on ahead so that their finishing power would not arouse suspicion. They may have thought that Jack had gone back to the ground to wait for us, but he was standing at the top of the hill and had seen the whole show. When we did get back to the ground, he had the boys in and gave them a stern lecture.

Scunthorpe might be a stock joke at working men's clubs, but, contrary to what people might imagine, it is a clean, neat town. The steelworks, which are not a pretty sight, are on the outskirts. I enjoyed my time at Scunthorpe and missed the place for a long time after I went to Liverpool.

As an apprentice, I would be up at eight o'clock in the morning to get to the Old Show Ground by nine o'clock. Sometimes I caught a bus, while other times I would walk. It took only fifteen to twenty minutes and was a pleasant stroll. In the mornings we would clean the boots, sweep out the passages, lay out the kit and empty the rubbish

Waiting for Shanks, May 1971.

Short back and sides, Scunthorpe fashion.

With Lennie and friends.

Man in a suitcase at Lilley Road.

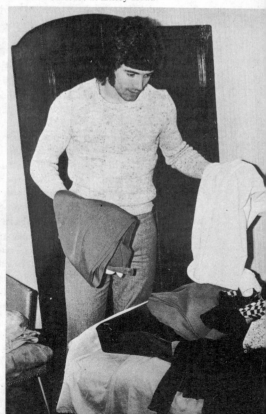

from the previous day. We also ran baths for players who were having treatment for injuries. Then we joined the other players for training and would be responsible for taking the equipment. We trained at a place called Quibell Park, travelling there in a minibus. It was a mile there and two miles back. The old bus, weighed down with gear, could manage the downhill journey from the ground, but the hills were too steep on the way back and we had to make a detour.

Oddly enough, we never saw a soccer goal-post until we played a proper match. This was because there were only two playing pitches at Quibell Park, one for rugby and the other for hockey. Imagine the first team goalkeeper in the rugby goals, with a crossbar nine feet from the ground. The lads could just chip the ball over his head, but when Saturday came their shots went high into the crowd! Even I was a world beater in the little hockey nets.

Sometimes, if the bus was overloaded or a couple of players had arrived on trial, the apprentices would have to run back to the ground. In the afternoons, when the other players had gone home, our work really began. 'The toilets need cleaning,' Jack would tell us or he would say, 'We're having trouble with a turnstile at the other side of the ground,' and we would carry our tools over and try to mend it. I will attempt anything, although I do not have much technical ability. I know many people who are brilliant with their hands, who would love to play football. I used to envy Jack, because he was good at everything technical and could repair anything.

When we had finished our chores we would go to a café four hundred yards from the ground and play the pinball machines. We played the machines so often that we discovered ways of shaking them to get the balls back without paying. After countless free plays we would say, 'Watch for the little hand coming out with the white flag to surrender.'

I was in digs with Mrs Ruby Duce in Edward Street, the house where Ray Clemence stayed before his transfer to Liverpool. Mel Blyth, who went on to win an FA Cup winners' medal for Southampton against Manchester United, was in digs next door, at Mrs Ida Baker's house. Mrs Baker had a beagle called Pharaoh, or 'Fezz' as we nicknamed him. Fezz was a pest and we hated him. Usually, I like animals, but I need to feel that they mean something in life, which Fezz did not. He simply existed, and was fat and lazy. Fezz had a habit of sitting on Mel's chair. When Mel came into the room and saw the dog resting, he would pick him up by the ears, drop him to the floor, and half-volley him with his left foot. It is no secret that Mel's left foot came on strongly while he was with Scunthorpe, and Fezz deserves credit for that!

Mel told me, 'Mrs Baker will ask you to take it for a walk, and when she does, run it round the block and it will never come near you again.' But I was the new boy, and when Mrs Baker asked me to take Fezz for a walk, that is exactly what I did. It was quite a struggle, because the dog was so lazy it could hardly stand up. Mel was not pleased with me. When the dog was becoming a nuisance, I decided to give him a run round the block – over the final two hundred yards Fezz was sliding along on his belly with his legs outstretched. When I stopped, he sat down and refused to go any further, and I had to drag him home. I would not have minded so much if Fezz had been old, but he wasn't. He was just totally uninterested in anything except sleeping on Mel's chair.

When some players join Liverpool it takes them months to get fit – what Liverpool call being 'super-fit' – but when I arrived I am certain I was as fit as any player Liverpool had on their books. That is what Scunthorpe did for me. Jack Brownsword was a hard coach who believed that if you were fit you could run for ninety minutes – whether or not you could play was another matter! We did a fair amount of work with a ball in training, but not enough. In fact, we used to ask, 'What are those round things in that bag, Jack?' Some Monday mornings, after a bad defeat the previous Saturday afternoon, we were not likely to see a football at all!

We used to play to crowds of around 3000, but though attendances were small there was a good atmosphere at Scunthorpe, and I think the supporters took to me. Most English crowds will encourage a trier. If the Scunthorpe fans were upset about a player's performance, they would let him know about it. At Liverpool, the occasional jibe from the crowd is usually drowned by the rest of the din, but at Scunthorpe every word came over loud and clear. I have heard shouts of, 'Keep out of the pubs and concentrate on your football!' directed at players.

Sometimes players gave vent to their feelings, such as Barry Jackson, the York City centre half, who was sent off during a match at the Old Show Ground. I was substitute for the game and was sitting in the dugout alongside Jack Brownsword. As Jackson came off the pitch, he started cursing. I think he was more annoyed with himself than anyone else. For some reason, Scunthorpe provided only one bucket of water to be shared by the trainers of both clubs – perhaps they thought no two players would be injured at the same time – which was placed between the two dugouts. When Jack and I told him to get off, Jackson kicked the bucket into our dugout. We were soaked, and though we laugh about it now, Jack was very angry indeed at the time.

When we could get together for an afternoon, Jack and I would take on Nige Cassidy and another team mate, Terry Heath, at foursomes golf. Terry was quite good, Nige wasn't bad, Jack would hit the ball a long way but struggled on the greens and I was learning the game. Jack and I had been beaten twice, and were delighted to be three holes up with four to play in the third game. It looked as though it could be our come-back match. I drove and hit a good shot, the ball landing on the fairway, which was most unusual for me in those days. Jack had hit one of his 'yellow perils' – a yellow coloured ball we swore was rubber because it bounced a hundred yards after hitting the fairway. Terry had played his drive, and we were just waiting for Nige. He decided to take an iron instead of a wood, and the rest of us walked along the tee while he lined it up. Nige swung his club into a full-blooded drive, the ball flying past my nose and hitting Terry on the chin. Amazingly, it did not knock Terry out, but he was extremely dizzy and we could not find the ball. We thought it might have embedded itself in Terry's head. Jack was convinced the whole thing had been planned so Nige and Terry could call off the game when we stood to win a couple of pounds off them! Ever since then I have made a point of standing well behind any player about to drive off a tee.

As a less hazardous pastime, Jack and I would play Nige and Terry at cards during coach journeys to away matches. We played partner whist, a game in which the high cards take the tricks. Jack and I rarely lost. The stake would be ten pence, whereas at Liverpool I played for a pound and sometimes a fiver. Jack had a habit, expecially if the game was not going well for us, of shuffling the cards by throwing them against the window of the coach. He would then scramble the cards together and count them, saying, 'That will have shuffled them up.' Nine times out of ten, we were dealt a better hand, so it became a tradition.

On one away trip to play at Workington, things were not going well for Jack and me. Nige and Terry had just beaten us 13–0 and Jack was not pleased. As usual, he gathered up the cards and threw them against the window, forgetting that it was open. The coach was moving at about sixty miles per hour and the cards were sucked out, disappearing in the slipstream. Jack could only gaze in disbelief at the five cards that remained on the table while the rest of us doubled up with laughter. We bought another pack of cards in Workington for the journey home.

Once I had settled at Scunthorpe, I wanted to buy a car. An uncle had a Morris 1100, and I decided that was what I would look for, even though I had been warned off them. 'Can't get parts for the engine ... nothing but trouble,' people would say. The more people advised me against an 1100, the more determined I became to get one – my stubborn streak again. I still sent Mum home whatever money I could afford, but I had started to save small amounts from my bonuses, and one day I saw a blue Morris 1100, priced at £365, which I thought I could afford. I went for a test drive and liked it, so I put down £100 and paid the rest on HP. It was nothing but trouble. By the time I had finished having parts replaced it was a new car except for the body-work, which was starting to rust. It also needed a respray, but I could not afford to pay £60 or £70 to have the job done. That was when two of the players decided to help me out. Ray Holt, who had moved to Scunthorpe from Halifax, and Mervyn Friar, who was signed from local football, said they were going into the car business as body repairers.

They offered to do it for £25, a week's wages for me then, including appearance money and bonuses, but I thought it would be worth it, having spent so much money on the rest of the car. I let them take it, and the car was gone for four days. I happened to be staying with my parents in Doncaster that particular week, and when the car was ready, Ray and Mervyn drove it over to me. They arrived in the evening when it was pitch black, and under the street lights my old 1100 looked fabulous. I paid and thanked them, went for a short drive and then went to bed, well contented. In those days that car was my life.

When I looked at it again next morning I thought someone had been denting it with hammers. Where the paint had not run it was thickly plastered over pock-marks. The only familiar thing was that it was blue. I could not believe how bad it looked in daylight, having seen it the night before. Although Dad knew nothing about cars, I asked him to have a look at mine. He barely knew one end from the other, and did not know how to start one. He had spent his life travelling on trams and buses. When he did get into a car he would just sit there and tell me where to take him. But he took one look at the resprayed 1100 and said, 'When you get to that bloody club, tell those lads that they could get jobs spraying oranges for Outspan.'

I have never seen anything quite as knobbly as that car. I never let Ray and Mervyn live it down. Even when I met them later I would sound off about it, and we would have a good laugh. If anyone at the club felt gloomy about life they would go outside and laugh at my car. Even the car rejected its new coat. In spite of all the money I had spent on the engine, it still gave me trouble. Finally, I literally pushed it to a garage in the hope of trading it for a new car – a smart, maroon Cortina. When I showed the 1100 to the salesman in Doncaster, he asked me, 'Who sprayed this then?'

'A couple of mates of mine,' I replied.

'Mates have done this?' he said. 'Are you sure they are mates?'

The Cortina cost £890 and I was offered £250 for my old car. Mum and Dad loaned me £500, which was their life savings, and I made up the rest myself. The Cortina was the envy of most of the lads at the club – with only 8000 miles on the clock, I made what turned out to be a good investment. I also learnt the hard way that you only get what you pay for.

Inflation was beginning to catch up with me. In the close season at Scunthorpe my basic £20 was whittled down after tax to a take-home pay of £14. I found it difficult to keep myself and run a car, and I decided to look for a summer job. I went to the Appleby Frodingham steelworks in Scunthorpe and discovered that the only way I could ge a job which paid reasonably well was to join a platelaying gang on the firm's railway line. Some of the older players were given easy jobs at the works, but, being seventeen, I was classed as a junior. If I had not joined the platelayers it would not have been worth taking a job at the steelworks.

At the end of each season I would move back to Doncaster to live with my parents, and had to get up at six o'clock in the morning in order to arrive at the works for 7.30. During my first week, one of the gangers asked, 'Are you a good worker, son?'

'Well I think so . . .' I replied.

'Look,' said the ganger, 'the first thing you do is find a place to sleep in the afternoons. Find a cubby-hole.'

When I realized he was being serious, I began to look for suitable quarters. I poked my head into a number of 'cubby-holes' before I eventually found somewhere to sleep or play cards in the afternoons. I had to do this, because if I had carried on working the bosses would have wondered where everyone else had gone. People who resented the fact that we were paid for playing football used to say, 'You should go to the steelworks and see what it's like there!' Having worked at the steelworks I could tell them about the cubby-hole system.

Players in the Third and Fourth Divisions are worse off financially than many industrial workers, a fact many spectators seem to overlook when they sneer at a lad who has had a bad game. Players in the lower divisions have to love the game, because the rewards are small and they have to put up with the drawback of constantly being in the public eye. When things go well, everyone is happy. When they don't, the players are criticized.

I disliked the travelling involved in working at the steelworks, and the following close season I took a job as head porter at a mental hospital in Doncaster. I was wary of the patients at first, as most people are, but soon found there was no harm in them. There was a special ward for handicapped children, and I loved the kids in there. When

A moment's rest.

some people see spastic children they react by muttering 'poor things', but these kids do not want sympathy. They know only too well they are physically abnormal, but are happy in their own way. They want to be treated naturally. If you offer them sympathy they feel you are being false.

These children, though handicapped, are often still very strong. There was a boy at school called Billy, whose legs were bent. He used to waddle along and, though Billy could obviously never play football, he loved the game and was a keen spectator. Sometimes he would lose his balance and fall heavily on the ground. 'He must have broken something,' we thought, but Billy would just get up again and continue on his way. He was as hard as nails. Once, when I had not long known him, I saw that he was about to fall and put my hands out to stop him. Billy was so strong that when his hands landed on my shoulders he pushed me over, falling on top of me, and I was pinned to the ground. Billy did not have much strength in his legs, but was amply compensated in his shoulders and arms. When I have finished with professional football I would like to find the time to work with handicapped children and help them to use their special strengths to enable them to lead more interesting and useful lives.

Some of the patients at the hospital were allowed to go into town at weekends, and would save money to buy things to brighten their days. Anything mechanical seemed to fascinate them. One lad paid £20 for a record player with twin speakers. He had a fad about cigarette lighters, owning a whole collection of them, of all shapes and sizes. They were his most prized possessions.

'Did you go shopping on Saturday?' I asked him one day.

'Yes,' he said. 'Just wait until you see what I got.' And off he ran to his room, urging me to stay where I was.

'Look at this, mister,' he said when he returned, full of excitement. 'I got two more lighters!'

One of them was distinguished by a picture of Blackpool Tower and the other was made of cheap metal, although my friend insisted, 'It's gold, mister.'

'How much were they?' I asked, out of curiosity.

'Nothing.'

'Someone gave them to you. That's nice.'

'No. They didn't cost me anything because I swopped my record player and speakers for them.'

'Didn't you get any money as well?'

'No, mister, I didn't have to give any money.'

'But didn't you *get* money?' I pressed, beginning to realize what had happened. He was delighted with his new toys, but someone in town had taken advantage of him by taking his record player and speakers in exchange for two lighters worth no more than eight shillings. I thought that was scandalous. It served to show me how vulnerable some people can be.

The patient was one of my three helpers, and I had to keep an eye on them all the time. For instance, when I first arrived I was shown around the hospital and told which wards had diabetic patients, so I could plan accordingly when delivering the food. My helpers tended to shove all the food packs on to the trolley and I had to stop them to reorganize matters. During my first couple of weeks there would be panic calls from the wards. The food for the diabetics had managed to find its way elsewhere. Sometimes I was as absent-minded as my helpers. I was given an old electric milk truck, on which to transport goods round the hospital. I would walk at the front, holding down the long handle to put the truck in motion, and lifting the handle to brake.

One sunny day my helpers and I were taking the truck down the side of the building. I breezed along in front, holding the handle and thinking what a wonderful world it was. Suddenly, there was a great crashing sound from behind me, and I turned to see that a window frame had been torn from the building with a smashing of glass and a pounding of bricks and cement. While daydreaming, I failed to notice that one of the windows, with a sky blue frame, had been left open, and had guided the truck straight into it. The helpers thought it was great fun. They shrieked with delight until just about everyone in the hospital had arrived to look at the rubble and laugh at the dent in my truck. On another occasion, I managed to spill a fifty-six-pint churn of milk all over the floor.

When it came time for me to leave the hospital and collect my cards, the recruiting officer, who was only a young man himself, wished me all the best. Then he said, 'I've been sitting with this paper, working out how much you've cost us in the short time you've been here – and we're not sorry to see you go back to Scunthorpe!'

6

Little white lies

In September 1970, while Lester Piggott and Nijinsky were winning racing's triple crown with a triumph in the St Leger, Kevin Keegan and his friend Phil Niles were chatting up a couple of girls at the Leger Fair. I had known Phil since schooldays, and after wandering around the fairground looking at the swings, roundabouts and sideshows, we paused near the waltzers. The girls were shouting and screaming as they whirled around, and Phil and I began to laugh at them. When the waltzer stopped and they climbed out, Phil and I took it over, and the girls got their own back by laughing at us. We stayed on for three trips, after which we must have been green in the face. When we had finished we wandered over to the girls and introduced ourselves. Their names were Jean Woodhouse and Wendy Devlin.

We talked for a while and then one of us said, 'Would you like to go for a drink?' The girls looked at us and then at each other before saying, 'We don't drink.'

'We mean for an orange juice or something,' I said. I was then nineteen and Jean just sixteen.

The two of us took Jean and Wendy to a pub called the 'Silver Link'. They had orange juice while Phil and I drank coke or shandy and tried to impress them with a non-stop barrage of jokes. The girls said they had to be home by ten o'clock, and insisted on catching a bus, although we did persuade them to let us drive them to their bus stop.

'I like the car,' said Jean as we approached my Cortina; 'is it yours?'

'No,' I said, 'it's my Dad's.' I did not want her to think I was showing-off.

As we drove along, Phil and I continued to pour out our jokes, and as we all seemed to be getting along very well, I said, 'We might as well take you on home now.' I had halted at traffic lights, when the girls climbed out of the car and ran away. They were determined that we should not take them home. After that we did not expect to see them again.

Shortly before Christmas, Phil and I took two other girls dancing at the Top Rank in Doncaster. We left them near the dance floor while we went to buy drinks, and as we walked along the balcony I heard some say, 'Hello, Phil, Hello, Kev.' We turned to find two girls looking towards us. One of them was smiling, and I was trying to place her when she said, 'You don't remember me, do you?' It was Jean, but the girl with her was not Wendy, who had apparently started courting, but another friend, Anne Skidmore. Before we rejoined our partners, Phil and I arranged to date Jean and Anne the following night. We took them to a pub, 'Annie's Arms', not far from Jean's home, a fish and chip shop at Carcroft. Apparently, Anne said to Jean, 'I fancy Kev more than Phil,' while Jean said, 'I like them both, so you chat up Kev and I'll talk to Phil.'

I was asked about my job, and said 'I ... work at Scunthorpe ... at the ... at the steelworks.' I did not want them to know I was a footballer. Jean and Anne were, at that stage, just a couple of girls we were dating, but I felt that it was better to let them get to know me for what I was as a person rather than to try a make a big impression. Not that I was a star, but I had heard other footballers making a big thing of it. I always felt that this created a false friendship by forcing an image on to people.

Jean was studying for her 'A' Levels (she passed in German and Economics) at Percy Jackson Grammar School and was secretary of the school youth club. One night, when I knew there was a dance at the school, at which Jean would be collecting tickets on the door, I went to see her. I made it appear that I was making a noble gesture and clearing the way for Phil, but really I fancied Jean for myself. 'I know you fancy Phil a lot, and I've come to arrange things so that you two can go out together without bothering about me and Anne,' I said. Jean said what I wanted to hear: 'It's not that I fancy Phil any more than you, but Anne fancies you and I just...' We smiled at each other, and from that moment we began to go out together. Anne was more serious about her studies and went on to take a degree course. Phil took a course in physical education and became a teacher in Manchester, and Wendy eventually married her economics teacher.

I was travelling from Scunthorpe to date Jean and she still thought I worked at the steelworks, but after about three weeks she put me on the spot by asking me to go ice skating on a Saturday afternoon.

'Sorry, I can't ... I'm going out somewhere,' I said.

'Oh yes – got somebody else, have you?' said Jean.

I decided it was time to tell her that I was a professional footballer. I do not like telling lies, not even little white ones, but I was beginning to tell one to cover up another. She accepted my explanation, understanding that I did not want her to think I was a big-head. I did not want to feel that she only went out with me because I was a footballer.

It was about this time that headlines began to appear in the local papers: 'NEWCASTLE WANT KEEGAN!' Then it was Sunderland, Leicester City, Sheffield Wednesday and Millwall. On and on went the list of names. I read that Arsenal wanted to take me on tour and that Preston had offered £5000 less than the club would accept. Every club in the League seemed to be after me, but I was kept in the dark. Some of it was just newspaper talk, but the manager never told me anything. That was probably because I was young and he wanted me to keep my feet on the ground. I played at Goodison Park against Tranmere Rovers in a replayed League Cup tie. I was still a midfield player then, and thought I had a good game. The newspapers said Everton were after me, but nothing happened.

Months passed and, in spite of all the headlines, nothing materialized. I became frustrated, then depressed. Scunthorpe had given me my chance in professional football when Coventry City had turned me down. I had gained invaluable experience and was grateful to them, but I had become unsettled. The headlines had led me to expect a transfer to a bigger club, and I began to long for something to change my routine. I became bored and thought of quitting football. I even considered going back to Peglers.

Eventually I told Jack Brownsword that I would not be coming back for the following season. 'Stick it out, son,' replied Jack. 'Don't worry. Within two months you will be with a First Division club.' I was sceptical. 'It's right,' said Jack. 'I know Leeds are very interested – Don Revie is on the phone to me about you a lot.' That was not true. Don Revie told me later that it was Jack who had phoned him and said, 'If you want a good player, he'll give you a hundred per cent effort and will force his way into your team.' Don made no move for me, yet later he picked me for England and chose me to captain the team.

Jack was determined to lift my spirits. But for him I think I would have given up. And Jack was right – within two months I *was* with a First Division club.

7

Shanks is waiting

I was sitting on a dustbin outside the temporary offices of Liverpool Football Club when three or four photographers arrived. 'Can I take a picture of you sitting there?' asked one. 'Well, they are signing a load of rubbish, so people might as well know it straight away,' I joked. There was nowhere else for me to sit. The interior of the club's new main stand had not been completed and the whole place was as busy as you might expect it to be with the team less than a week away from playing in an FA Cup Final at Wembley.

It was May 1971, and Scunthorpe had agreed to transfer me for a fee of £33,000. Ron Ashman, who travelled with me to clinch the deal, was becoming somewhat agitated. He was not too happy with the reception. I was his best player, his most prized possession, and he was selling me. He was pleased to be doing that, but expected me to get VIP treatment. I realized, however, that this was a different world. To Ron, I was a major player, but to Liverpool I was only a small cog about to be fitted into their machine.

I came to Liverpool's notice through Andy Beattie, Bill Shankly's great friend and former teammate, and Jack Brownsword, who had known Peter Robinson, the Liverpool secretary, when he held a similar position at Scunthorpe. It was an important day for me, and I bought a new white shirt and a red tie. 'Oh, red and white,' someone said, as if I was trying to make a good impression. Quite honestly, I had not been thinking about Liverpool's colours when I bought them.

I sat on the dustbin for twenty minutes after the photographers had left. I had heard of Shankly, of course, but he had not meant much to me at Scunthorpe. I wondered what to expect, but was not overawed. It was not until a couple of years later that I fully realized just what the man meant on Merseyside. When he came out of the door, he shook our hands and said, 'Medical!' Leaving Ron to have a cup of tea with Peter Robinson, he beckoned me over to his car, a Capri, and off we went. 'You'll like the stadium son. Great ' He was driving the car while half-looking round at me. 'Great supporters you know, son. The best in the land. Tremendous to play for. Have you seen the Kop? No, I don't suppose you have.' I never got the chance to say anything. 'We have got some great players here, son. Great ... great. Emlyn Hughes ... great player. Chris Lawler ... great player. Tommy Smith ... hard boy. Hard boy is Tommy ... great player. Roger Hunt is gone, son. Ian St John is gone. But they're not forgotten, son. There is a future here if you knuckle down and play.'

We arrived at the club doctor's surgery and I stripped off. Shankly watched me like a hawk. My blood pressure, usually normal, was high. It must have been the excitement, because the doctor checked it again a couple of days later as a precaution and it was back to normal. When he said the pressure was high I became a little worried. Transfers have fallen through because players have not passed Liverpool's standards of medical fitness. One such player was Freddie Hill, of Bolton, and later there was the case of Frank Worthington, who eventually signed for Leicester City. But I think Shanks was keen to sign me from the moment he saw my build, particularly the way the weight training had developed my shoulders. When we left the doctors he drove me back to the ground to talk over terms.

As he drove, he talked of the time when he first came to the club. 'Jesus Christ,' he began. 'I asked a wee boy for directions and he knew who I was, and I'd only been in Liverpool half-an-hour!' He obviously could not wait to get me training. When we arrived back at Anfield and walked into the temporary offices, I could hear him talking way ahead of me. Talking the way he always did – so everyone could hear, especially the person who was the subject of his conversation. 'He looks nothing dressed, but you should see him stripped off. He's built like a tank!'

When we reached the manager's office, Ron Ashman and Peter Robinson were waiting for us. 'Right, terms, son,' said Shankly. 'We can offer you £45 a week.' I wanted to sign there and then but remembered that my father had told me not to sell myself cheap. 'Oh . . . I thought I would be getting more than that,' I said. 'That's upsetting,' said Shankly. 'Don't forget, young man, we're paying £33,0000 for you.' He started talking again about the 'great club, great crowd and great stadium'. 'Think of the opportunity,' he said. 'It's not what you get now that counts, it's what you get later.' I felt that I was worth £50. At Scunthorpe my basic had been £30 plus £8 for a win and £4 for a draw. That was in the Fourth Division. Here I was, about to move to the First Division and facing what I thought would be a fairly long fight to get into the first team.

'Yes, but I am a bit disappointed with the terms, Mr Shankly,' I said, 'because – and I don't want you to think I am being cheeky – I am nearly getting that much at Scunthorpe, and they are in the Fourth Division. I must better myself.' I expected him to shout at me, and Ron Ashman groaned, as if he could see £33,000 suddenly floating away from Scunthorpe. 'All right son. Fifty pounds,' said Shankly, and I picked up a pen and signed. As I did so, he added, 'If you do it for me, son, you will never have to ask for a rise,' and I never did. He kept his word right to the end.

Before the start of one season he had all the players in and out of his office in ten minutes, which is all it took for them to negotiate new contracts. 'What do you think you should get?' he would ask. The player would indicate how much he wanted. 'Well, I'm giving you more. How's that?' he would say. I popped my head round his office door and he told me, 'I'm doubling your wages.' 'Thank you,' I said, and that was that. It took less than twenty seconds. The same thing happened over and over again. He kept doubling my pay. He even made sure it was doubled again before he left the club.

When I had signed, he shook my hand and said, 'Welcome to the club. We'll give you time to get your things sorted out, son. Be here on Wednesday morning at 9.00 am.'

I only had a day to settle my affairs at home and find new digs. As soon as I arrived, he had me training. He played against me in five-a-side matches between the training staff and the players. As the staff were getting on in years and could not run most of the young lads tended to push the ball square, but I took on Shankly and the rest, performing cheeky tricks, such as knocking the ball to one side of them and running round the other side to meet it. I was trying to impress them.

I took Jean to London for the Cup Final, but I was so new to the club that I did not feel involved. I even found it hard to work up a strong feeling for Liverpool, but the faces of the players after losing 2-1 to Arsenal in extra time told me what it was like to lose a big match. Jean and I stayed at the Waldorf Hotel. Jean had a room on the third floor and I was on the fifth floor. We arranged that whoever woke up first in the morning would call the other. Next morning, I duly went down and knocked on Jean's door. When there was no reply, I thought she must have gone up to my room, but when I went back upstairs there was no sign of her. I went back down to Jean's room and asked the chambermaid to unlock the door, thinking she might have overslept. She was not there, so I went down for breakfast, expecting to find her at a table. After a while, Jean did appear, and asked me where I had been. It transpired that our lifts had been passing each other. Jean had also asked a chambermaid to unlock my door, fearing I might have been ill.

Roger Hunt was the only player to speak to me, something I shall never forget. Everyone else was too busy preparing for the Final. Roger had left Liverpool and was playing for Bolton Wanderers, but naturally he was invited to the Final. At the Waldorf Roger came up to me and said, 'Hello, pleased to meet you, I'm Roger Hunt,' as down to earth as could be. 'You've joined a great club, son, and if you try hard you'll make it, because the fans and everybody are great.' He probably sensed that I felt a little left out and somewhat lost in London that day, and in one sentence that fellow made me feel more at home than anyone else had done.

Signing for Liverpool had turned my whole world upside down. The fee of £33,000 was modest in terms of the current transfer market but it still sounded a vast amount of money to me. It had been a good move, I thought, believing that I would have to work my way up through the reserves. Not even Shanks in his wildest dreams could have thought he was signing me for his first team then. He signed me because he thought I had ability and in two or three years' time I might force my way through.

When I came to Liverpool, Jean was still at school. Liverpool seemed a million miles away to her. I was at the start of a new challenge and we were far too young to be making definite plans for the future. There was probably a perfectly simple and logical answer to our problem, but we could not fathom it. The easy way out would have been to break up but we did not want to do that. All we seemed to do was argue around the subject. Jean bought me a sad record, Diana Ross's 'Remember Me', which annoyed me because I had no intention of forgetting her. Although I was not seeking a lasting relationship with anyone, I had begun to feel that Jean might be the girl for me.

We tried to talk things over sensibly as we walked around Doncaster town centre one evening, but, as usual, we ended up bickering and eventually Jean walked away from me. I followed her and said, 'Get into the car and I'll take you home.' 'No,' she replied. 'I'll get the bus,' and off she went.

I thought that was the finish of it, and wrote to Jean saying how sorry I was at the way everything had turned out between us and that she could keep the records we had bought. Apparently the point about the records gave Jean the impression that the break-up was final as far as I was concerned, and she decided she would like to say goodbye, face to face. Jean came round to my parents' home. She was wearing a white blouse and a white mini-skirt, and I thought she was on her way to play tennis. We sat on the grass in the bullring and this time there was no argument between us. We agreed to continue our friendship, to write to each other and to see each other when we could. It was decided to let events take their course.

My first year at Liverpool must have been terrible for Jean. Everything was building up for me and she must have wondered whether I would change as a person. She wrote every day, posting the letters on her way to school. When I was able to go home, I would meet her from school, parking my car near the gates and teasing Jean by saying, 'You've got some nice girls at your school, haven't you?' We often met in Manchester on Sundays. Jean would catch a train from Doncaster and I would drive along the East Lancashire Road from Liverpool. We enjoyed those days together, but it was no way to get to know each other properly because we were so determined to make the most of the little time we had that it held back any conversation which might have led to an argument. We made sure everything ran smoothly, knowing we would not see each other again for at least a week.

One day, I telephoned her to ask if she was coming over. She said yes. 'I'll see you at the Golden Egg,' I told her. For some stupid reason, which I can only put down to forgetfulness, I thought Jean was coming to Liverpool. I never used to meet Jean in Liverpool, but on this occasion I went to the Golden Egg restaurant in Liverpool and Jean went to the Golden Egg restaurant in Manchester. After waiting for some time, I telephoned Jean's mother to ask if she had left. I was told that she had, so I waited a little longer and then it suddenly clicked – Manchester! I jumped into my car and drove to Manchester, but there was no sign of Jean at the Golden Egg. I telephoned Jean's mother again and discovered that she had not returned home. Jean arrived home twenty minutes later. She caught a train to Doncaster about the time I was setting off from Liverpool.

Just as I did at Scunthorpe, I moved into digs vacated by Ray Clemence. This time my address was The Nook, Lilley Road, in the Prescot Road area of Liverpool, and my landlady was Mrs Lindholme. Liverpool ensured I was kept busy. I trained again the week after the Cup Final, and in mid-May was one of sixteen players chosen for a twelve-day tour of Scandinavia. The tour helped me settle quickly with my new team mates, making me feel I was a good enough player to be in their company. Our first game was at Arhus and we were beaten 3–2. I thought this was my fault, because Liverpool just did not lose matches like that. I was soon to learn that while a pre-season tour is taken seriously, because the club is preparing for the forthcoming League campaign, the end-of-season tour is treated as something of a joke. Bill Shankly believed he had more important work to do back home and remained in Liverpool. All the lads treated everything lightheartedly – except me. I was trying to impress and to prove myself as a player.

I wore a number eight jersey in that first game, and played in midfield. Liverpool had seen me playing in a retreating wing position, similar to Ian Callaghan, at Scunthorpe, and they believed they had signed a midfield player. We then played at Lulea, which reminded me of a cowboy town. All the houses were made of wood and lager cost some £2 a can. As we rolled into town on our bus, some of the boys, in holiday mood, shouted, 'Look – a beach!' The interpreter tapped his microphone at the front of the bus and put us right: 'Gentlemen, zat is ice.' We had forgotten how close we were to the Arctic Circle. It was a rather bleak town, and there were more bicycles than cars. The interpreter's first words to us were, 'Pleased to meet you, but why on earth have you come to Lulea?'

The answer was Liverpool's popularity in Scandinavia. The football followers there see many of our matches on television and send us a weight of mail during the course of a season. We won the match 5–0, and I scored the first goal – my first goal for Liverpool. I cannot recall it in detail. I vaguely remember playing a 'one–two' move with a team mate and then, as the goalkeeper came out, pushing the ball past him. From Lulea we moved on to our most important match of the tour, at Sundsvall. We won 4–0 and I scored the second goal. A local committee also selected me as man of the match and I was presented with a bronze statuette. I was still a little wary, after moving from Scunthorpe, where at least I knew how I stood and where people had begun to respect me for what I could do, and the game in Sundsvall helped enormously. Though still treading cautiously, I was taking on a little more responsibility and increasing my work rate. I could surmise from the attitude of some of the other players that they were beginning to think I could play.

After the tour we had a short break, reporting back for training during the second week of July. The first team squad went on a pre-season tour abroad, but I stayed home with the reserves. Ronnie Moran was left in charge. Our first pre-season match was against the Tranmere Rovers first team at Prenton Park. The previous season, I had played in three tough Cup matches against Tranmere for Scunthorpe, eventually beating them 1–0 at Goodison Park. Here I was playing against Tranmere again, for Liverpool reserves. During the Cup games, Johnny King and I had given each other a hard time. He had been marking me and we both had a few bruises to show for it. I think Johnny was still sore about Scunthorpe winning, and when the match started, we carried on from where we had left off. I thought I was playing quite well and was pleased with the way I was handling Johnny King, not an easy player to be up against, but when I went into the dressing-room at half-time. Ronnie Moran immediately started on me.

'What the hell do you think you're doing? You're not playing like a Liverpool player.'

'What do you mean?' I said, completely taken aback.

'You're just free and easy,' he replied. 'You're just charging about the midfield. You're nearly playing up front. You're a midfield player – you've got responsibilities defensively as well as in attack!'

For a while I felt disillusioned, because this was the way I had always played in midfield – carefree and easy, something like Trevor Brooking plays for West Ham. He does not do much defensively. He always wants to go forward, which was exactly what I wanted to do. As a result, I received a good telling off, and I also thought Ronnie had it in for me. Most young lads feel that way when someone shouts at them. Now that I know Ronnie better and understand his character, I realize he was trying to help me. We had different ideas. Ronnie had a highly successful reserve team and was proud of it. He knew how he wanted his team to play and I did not fall in line with his idea of a midfield player. I still feel that the way I played then is the same style as I play now. Being more experienced, I probably would not charge about quite so much, but the way I play remains quite similar.

We beat Tranmere 2–1, the winning goal coming from a penalty awarded when I was chopped down. New Brighton were beaten in our next match, with me scoring another goal. The first team arrived back from their tour before my last pre-season game for the reserves, which was at Southport. Ronnie must have told Bill Shankly his feelings about my midfield play, and suggested that I should be given a game in the attack. That is exactly what happened at Southport, on 6 August, in a game we won 2–1. Shankly was watching, and I felt I had done everything a front man should do, including scoring our two goals. The first team was then finding difficulty in scoring goals. They were drawing matches 0–0 or only winning 1–0 with a scrappy effort, and this was worrying Shanks.

Four days later, Liverpool played their usual pre-season club match – first team versus reserves – behind closed doors, and I was picked for the first team. This took place on the Tuesday of the week leading up to the start of the League programme. Nine out of ten professionals will agree that the one team that inevitably beats them is their own reserve side. This is mainly because most first team players do not think they have anything to prove to the manager, while virtually all reserve players feel that they should be in the first team. When the first team plays the reserves there is always more incentive for the reserves to do well. When I saw my name in the first team attack for that game I honestly believed that, although Shanks said he was trying me out because he thought I had ability, it was more a case of him attempting to warn other players who were not doing so well, such as Bobby Graham and Alun Evans, who had both had a disappointing pre-season tour. It was probably just as well that I took this view, because I went into the game without any illusions.

We played at Melwood, the club's training ground, the spectators being just a knowledgeable few – Bill Shankly, Bob Paisley, his assistant, Reuben Bennett, the coach, Joe Fagan, the first team trainer, and Ronnie Moran, the reserve team trainer. It was like being back at the Old Show Ground, playing for Scunthorpe in front of a sparse crowd. Having said that, there is still an atmosphere in private club games. You can hear all the shouting – and there is plenty of it, on the field and off. Players get on with a game, whether or not there is a crowd watching. Shanks would always be heard shouting, 'Aw, Jesus, son! What are you doing?' 'Our Jeannette', Shanks's daughter, was mentioned constantly during practice matches. 'Our Jeannette could kick a ball further than that!' was a common cry. I used to giggle as I ran along with the ball, because I was still only learning Shankly's sayings. The match was a farce, rather like something you might read in 'Roy of the Rovers'. The first team won 7–1 with the ball flying all over the field. I scored a hat-trick, and although I have had some fine games for Liverpool and scored some good goals. I have never played another game like that one. I have never put it all together in one match like that. We just tore the heart out of the reserves. One of the reasons I played so well was that I wanted to make Ronnie Moran eat his words. I wanted to show him that I could play, because I did not think he rated me.

Afterwards, when we were having a cup of tea, a couple of the players told me, 'You'll be playing on Saturday after that – you've got to be.' While I thought I had done my chances a great deal of good, I was not expecting to get into the team straightaway. 'This is Liverpool,' I thought, 'they're not going to be convinced by a performance in one game.'

The following day Shanks came up to me and said, 'How are you enjoying it, son?'

'Fine,' I replied.

'Do you feel fit?'

'Yes.'

'Where do you want to play on Saturday – in the reserves or in the first team?'

I had already learned enough about the man to know how to answer him. 'Well, I haven't come here to play in your reserve side,' I said.

It must have been the right answer, because he said, 'Good, good, off you go and get a cup of tea, son,' and that was it. I was in the team on Saturday.

That conversation is typical of the man. Whenever a player was injured, he would say, 'How is it, son? Is it sore?'

'Well, it is a bit.'

'Is it easier today than it was yesterday?'

'Yes, it's getting better every day.'

'Was it easier yesterday than it was the day before that?'

'Er . . . yes . . . yes.'

'Then it will be easier tomorrow than it is today.' He would go the long way round in order to get you to say what he wanted you to say – to convince yourself that you were fully fit again.

I telephoned Dad and told him, 'I think I'll be playing, but I'll let you know for sure on Friday.' He was extremely excited, but I did not want him to set his heart on it until I had seen the team sheet. When I became established I stopped looking at the team sheet. I knew that if I was fit I would be playing. But I will never forget the excitement I felt that first time at Liverpool. In those days, when the main stand at Anfield was being completed, we used Melwood as a base, and the typewritten team sheet, signed by Shanks, was pinned up in the dressing-room: 'Liverpool v. Nottingham Forest . . . 7 – KEEGAN.'

It looked wrong. People have said to me, 'Kevin Keegan – it just sounds as if you made that name up to suit you.' But the name did not look at all right on that team sheet. I used to think, 'George Best – now there's a name that was meant to be famous. Rodney Marsh – that sounds like a footballer's name. But Kevin Keegan just doesn't sound right.' I suppose a name never sounds right at first. It is only when people use it continually that it becomes acceptable. Keegan looks right now, but when I first saw it in Shanks's team I felt as if it should not have been there. I telephoned Dad and Jean to confirm that I had been selected. The family decided to come over to Liverpool and make an outing of it. My brother Mike attended, as did my sister, Mary, who was married and living at Carcroft, where Jean comes from.

Normally, it took me about five minutes to drive from my digs to Anfield, but on the day of my big opportunity I completely overlooked the fact that more than 50,000 other people would be heading for the same destination. I was told to be at the ground for two o'clock, an hour before the kick-off, and left my digs at about 1.55, with Mum, Dad, Mike and Jean in my Cortina. There I was, trying to sneak through the enormous build-up of traffic, desperate to get to the ground to play in the biggest game of my life – and nobody knew me.

When I stopped and asked a policeman if he could help, he said, 'Why, where are you going?'

'I'm playing in the match!'

'Who for, Nottingham Forest?'

'No – Liverpool!'

'Don't give me that, son – pull the other one!'

I was directed first one way and then the other, and as I approached Anfield the scene reminded me of Wembley Way. Eventually, I managed to talk my way past the stewards guarding the main entrance. I had even left behind my ticket for the club car park, so I just put my car in the first available space, said a brief farewell to my parents and Jean, and dashed for the dressing-room, twenty-five minutes late. Shanks was pacing up and down the passageway, waiting for me. 'You should have been here twenty-five minutes ago, son. Go and get changed!' I can remember shuddering. When I walked into the dressing-room there were a few cracks from the players: 'Good of you to come' and 'We thought you might get here around half-time.' On reflection, being late was probably the best thing that could have happened to me. I did not have time to worry about anything. The dressing-room was sparkling new and my playing kit was all laid out neatly, with my boots placed underneath the bench. Before we left the dressing-room, Shanks told me to 'go out and enjoy it'. The lads wished me all the best, and I was ready for the big occasion.

I believe I can live with any situation in which I find myself. If I were going into the ring with Muhammad Ali tomorrow, I would honestly believe I deserved to be there. I would not think about being knocked out – though I am sure this would happen – but only of winning. That is the sort of person I am, not easily overawed. It explains how I was able to take in my stride the fact that I had just left Scunthorpe in the Fourth Division and was about to make my debut at Liverpool in the First Division, on the first day of a new season.

The reception was something special. The Liverpool players ran to the centre of the field and waved, in turn, to all parts of the stadium. This was traditional, before the first game of a season and at the end of the final match, but I did not really feel a part of it. I was still very much a stranger. After waving to the other parts of the ground, the players turned and faced the famous Kop. The ovation was deafening,

71

the red and white scarves and flags appearing to have a life of their own. The whole scene got through to me. I had never experienced anything like it, but I refused to be overawed. I was looking forward to the game and felt I was going to score.

The fans on the Kop chanted my name, 'Ke-vin Kee-gan ... Ke-vin Kee-gan'. It sounded as strange as it had looked on the Liverpool team sheet. No one had chanted my name before. They had just called me names! The self-appointed representative of the Kop came on to the field to greet me. He gave me a kiss, and the smell of booze on his breath almost knocked me off my feet. He needed a shave as well, for his beard was rough. The police accept this ritual whenever there is a new player. This Kopite is a nice, old fellow with no harm in him. He kissed me, then kissed the grass in front of the Kop and went back to join his mates in the crowd.

My job was to score goals or make them, and we had been playing for about thirteen minutes when Peter Thompson moved up the right wing. That was unusual in itself, because Peter mainly favoured playing on the left. He drove the ball across and it came to me, six yards out from goal towards the near post. I intended to blast the ball and break the roof of the net, but it skimmed off my boot and began to bobble. Jim Barron was in goal and the two full backs were on the line. The ball just rolled over one of the full back's feet for a goal. After that, everything went like a dream. Our second goal came when I was fouled, Tommy Smith scoring from the penalty. Emlyn Hughes scored our third goal, and Ian Moore converted a penalty for Forest to make the final score 3–1.

I have seen many players come and go in a short time. Moore was transferred to Manchester United and had to retire because of a bad injury. Peter Cormack, who became my closest friend at Liverpool and is now with Bristol City, played against us that day. Meanwhile Billy Bremner was making his 400th League appearance for Leeds United at Manchester City. Bremner is no longer at Leeds. They seemed glad to get rid of him in the end, when he was transferred to Hull City, but at the time I moved up into the First Division, he was in the driving seat at Leeds. Billy figures more prominently in my story later.

Encouraged by my goal, I gained confidence in that game against Forest. I was soon knocking the ball to one side of a player and running round the other side to meet it. I did many cheeky tricks with the ball. I ran all over the field, chasing balls I ought to have had no chance of getting, but sometimes I was successful. It was unbelievable. I thought about the contrast with Scunthorpe, and said to myself, 'It's easier up here!'

A touch of the Cossacks.

8

Football elbow

My first season at Liverpool was incredible. I can remember wanting each game to come quicker, and suddenly people were talking and writing about Kevin Keegan. The *News of the World* voted me 'Outstanding Goalscorer' for August, the *Sun* called me 'Whiz Kid' in November, and that same month I was the *Daily Mirror*'s 'Monday Man'. Sir Alf Ramsey selected me for my first England Under-23 cap in February 1972, and before the summer arrived I was voted Merseyside Footballer of the Year, Football League Review Young Footballer of the Year, Granada Television Player of the Year and Bargain Buy of the Year, and *Daily Express* Superstar. Liverpool finished third in the First Division, one point behind Derby County, the Champions, and pushed out of second place on goal average by Leeds United.

I have criticized the press and television from time to time, which I have felt quite justified in doing, but there is no doubt that they made people take notice of my name. Looking back, I think the main reason I won so many awards in that first season was that English football was crying out for a new face and a new talent. George Best was then at his peak at Manchester United, just before everything went wrong for him at Old Trafford, but the press and television were searching everywhere for other players who could be built into stars.

Many people helped me on my way, but only one person made me. That was Shanks. As soon as I joined up with him I started to become a player. He was perfect for me, because I am the type who likes to strive for personal targets, and Shanks would set them for me. He worked it all out after a month of watching me play for Liverpool. He knew where I fitted in, what I was going to do and what he had to do to get the best out of me.

After that month he said, 'You are going to be the greatest player in England.'

'You say that to everybody,' I replied.

'No, no,' he continued. 'I'm not saying you are going to be as good as Denis Law, but you are going to be one of the greatest players in Britain.'

It was weird the way Shanks had a knack of being able to make things happen. He would sometimes make a remark, which sounded silly for a man with his experience, but later what he had said would come true. He is a good judge of character and rarely proved wrong in his assessment of people. Immediately, he either likes someone or hates them. There is no middle ground with Shanks. When he makes up his mind about something he is hard to budge, as I soon discovered.

With the extra money from my transfer, I repaid my parents what they had loaned me to buy the Cortina. Being in the first team, I was adding an extra £80 in bonuses to my £50 basic. I decided to buy a new car, a Capri. Everything was going well, but after some dozen games I developed a niggling injury in my left foot, a persistent ache of the bone, and missed a match because of it. There was no sign of it getting better. Shanks went through his usual psychological reasoning until I did not know what to say for the best. If you made a mistake in giving an answer, he would jump on you, verbally. Eventually, he lost his patience and said, 'Jesus Christ, son – what is it?'

'I don't know, boss, but I do know I can't play on it. It hurts to walk, let alone to run or kick a ball with it.'

The specialist did not help. He told Bob Paisley, 'I've never seen anything like it. The only thing it can be is tennis elbow in his foot.'

Imagine Bob going back to Shanks and saying, 'They think it is tennis elbow in his foot.'

I was on the treatment table, and had electrodes from the treatment machine attached to my foot. The team was ready to go to a match at Stoke City, and Shanks was pacing up and down, spelling out what dreadful things would have befallen me had I missed a game with an injury like that when he was a player at Preston. He was like a police inspector with his questions.

'You've not been riding a bike, have you, son?'

'No.'

'You've not been skiing?' Where could I have gone skiing in Liverpool?

He gave me the impression that he did not think there was anything wrong with me; that I was skiving. Suddenly, he took the electrodes off my ankle and said, 'You're going with me to Stoke, son. Get on that bus!' In my view, he was insinuating that I was cheating. It was an insult. Even then, when I was just beginning to know Shanks, I respected him. Later, I came to respect him more than any other person in my life, with the exception of my father. Shanks never scared me the way he seemed to scare others. I am not cheeky, but I have always stood up for myself when I thought I was right. At that moment, I knew I was right, and told him, 'I'm going home to Doncaster. If you want me, that's where I'll be.' I put on my clothes and stormed out, leaving Shanks speechless – which did not happen to him very often.

I felt depressed, that I was being got at and that the world had fallen in on top of me. But when I arrived home, Dad told me straight, 'You've got a contract – get back there!' When I returned to the club, Shanks treated me as if nothing had happened. He knew I had been home, but he was prepared to overlook it. He never even mentioned it. I think he respected me for having had the audacity to stand up for myself even when I was not in a position to bargain. He could have turned round and said, 'All right, we don't want you if you don't want to play for Liverpool.' It took an incident like that to show him the type of person I was.

Liverpool had a goalless draw at Stoke, and I was fit again within a week or so, although the club took my car off me for a while. 'We've got to try and find out what's been wrong with your foot,' said Shanks. 'We don't miss a trick here.' Joe Fagan was sent to inspect my car. Shanks told the story about the time Peter Thompson had a knee injury and they finally put the cause of it down to air jetting on to the knee from

A balanced view against Ferencvaros in Budapest.

You can't win 'em all . . .

a little hole in Peter's car. Joe reported, 'The clutch is stiff, I had a hell of a job pressing it down.' Shanks decided that if big Joe Fagan had difficulty operating the clutch, then he had found the answer. 'That's it, son,' he said, 'You've not to go in your car again.' My Capri was up against the wall of the Anfield car park for five days, while I walked along cobbled stone streets from bus stop to bus stop, occasionally going over on my uncertain ankle. I must have been stupid to let them talk me into not using my car, but I had reached the point where I was willing to try anything to clear up the injury.

During the season I had to have a great many cortisone injections. I still get aches in my bones from time to time, which I put down to wear and tear. I have not had a cartilage operation, or anything like that, but obviously parts of my body have taken a hammering. God did not make people to be professional footballers. It was not His intention that they should be running, turning, twisting, jumping, falling and kicking with such intensity every day. When you punish your body excessively, you must expect some kind of reaction.

The two disagreements I had with Shanks, over terms on the day I arrived and concerning the injury shortly after I started playing for him, were the foundations of our relationship. I also had to be accepted by the players. I have often been proved wrong in my preliminary assessment of people, which turned out to be the case when I first met Tommy Smith. Tommy was Liverpool's captain when I came to Anfield, and in my first season I was given more publicity than he had received in all the years he had been with the club. Naturally, I expected some resentment from him and the other established players, and in my early days at Anfield Tommy and I did not get on very well together, to say the least.

There was the occasion when I came down for breakfast at a hotel during a pre-season tour of West Germany and Holland. I had ordered the same food as another player, and when the waiter arrived and put down a plate in front of me, I started to eat. 'That's not yours!' shouted Tommy, loudly enough for everyone else in the place to hear. 'Wait your turn – you're not as big as you think you are!' My reply, as I recall, was neither clever nor subtle, but I had made up my mind from the beginning that I would have to stand up to Tommy. He was trying to pull me down a peg or two. I gave as good as I got, otherwise I might not have got where I am today. I refused to allow myself to be intimidated in any way.

One day during training at Melwood, some strong words were exchanged by us, leading to a punch-up. I put up my fists, Tommy put up his fists, and we laced into each other. It was only a flurry of blows, Larry Lloyd moving in and stopping the fight before it got out of hand. Larry grabbed hold of me, as I continued to swing my arms and shout at Tommy Smith. Out of the side of my mouth I told him, 'Keep hold of me, for God's sake – don't let go of me,' knowing that otherwise 'Smidge' would have killed me.

It was not all aggravation. Smidge was not above using me at times. There was an occasion when a photographer from the *Sun* arrived with an offer of money for a picture session. Whoever appeared on the pictures with me would get a share of the cash. Smidge was not slow in taking me to the studio!

I began to think of Smidge as the club bully, but my first impressions of him were wrong. During the last couple of years we have had a great relationship. We have come to understand each other. I think he realized that all the publicity and commercialization I received was as a result of the way I was playing. Top-class footballers were obviously in demand for advertising. He began to understand that pressure from other people had pushed me up to where I was, and it was not any conscious effort on my part to show that I was a cut above everyone else at the club. My attitude towards Smidge changed, even though I have always answered him back when I thought he was wrong. I have grown to respect him enormously as a player. He was a great captain, never selfish, always battling for the boys and not just for himself. He always ensured that everyone had a fair share of the rewards that came the team's way.

As a player, Smidge has always been known as a hard man. This is a fallacy. He had one season in which he was over-zealous with opposing players and established a reputation, but he then spent the rest of his career being a very good player without getting the credit for it. People were scared of him, in the same way that they would be scared of someone who had once beaten them up. One beating and a person can walk the streets for years on the strength of his reputation as a hard man. No one could take liberties with Smidge, but I have seen him fouled so many times when he has gone for the ball and an opponent has given him a sneaky kick. Foreign players have done this on several occasions. Smidge goes in hard, but he goes for the ball. He has been injured himself more often than he has injured others. There are still players around who are wary of Smidge, such as Leighton James of Derby County. Smidge always made a point of saying 'Hello, Leighton!' before any match between the sides got under way.

Liverpool players have always appreciated Smidge's ability, but it took his performance in the 1974 FA Cup Final victory over Newcastle United to convince most outsiders that he was a skilful player. Our third goal was beautifully worked. I hit a long ball over to Smidge on the right, after which he interplayed magnificently with the other lads before crossing the ball for the thirteenth pass of the move. All I had to do was tap the ball into the net to finish it off.

Emlyn Hughes was another player who had made a name for himself before I arrived, eventually taking over from Smidge as captain. No one can take anything away from Emlyn as a player of power and drive but, like me, he has had several setbacks during his career. He was playing for Blackpool when Shanks signed him for £65,000 in 1967. Although only a kid joining the great Liverpool team of the 1960s, he played a year, settled in and became a regular member of that side. His career continued to improve, as did his enthusiasm. He got into the England Under-23 team and was then selected for the full England team. He was made captain of Liverpool and went on to captain England.

Suddenly, whether rightly or wrongly, Don Revie dropped Emlyn from the England squad, and I wondered if he had the character to ride that disappointment. Emlyn had been used to success and his personality was not attuned to failure. I felt sorry for him, but also knew that his attitude was not helping his cause. He was just crying about it and saying he should have been in the squad when I think he should have been doing something more positive about it. The only place a footballer can go to prove a manager wrong is the football field. I told Emlyn that the sooner he concentrated on playing and stopped making his bitterness apparent to Revie, the sooner he was likely to be back in the England side. 'You've got to force him to pick you because of your performances,' I told him. 'There's no good in feeling sorry for yourself and moping about it. Just play so well that people will say, "All right, Don Revie doesn't pick him, but he is still the best player." ' Eventually, before England's dreadful World Cup qualifying match in Italy in 1976 Revie did recall Emlyn. He decided he needed him again, but it was Emlyn's play, not his moaning, which earned him another chance.

Before I joined Liverpool, Steve Heighway was the player who attracted most publicity and agents. Like myself, Steve experienced a dramatic move to the First Division from obscurity. He was spotted while playing amateur football for Skelmersdale United. It was not long before Steve's name began to appear here, there and everywhere, and he found difficulty in separating his private life from his life as a player. On top of that, some of the other players became somewhat jealous, because they knew Steve's popularity meant greater financial rewards from outside the game. Steve was genuinely pleased when I became the focal point of attention. 'I'm glad you came, because you took the pressure off me,' he said.

I had not been at Liverpool long when England's World Cup winners from 1966 came to Anfield to play in Roger Hunt's testimonial game. England were one or two players short because of injuries and club commitments, and I was drafted into their team to play against my own. Bill Shankly stood in front of the Liverpool players and said he would lead out the best team in the world and Sir Alf Ramsey the second best team in the world. It was a strange experience for me, because I scored one goal and made another for Jeff Astle. Every time I touched the ball after that I was booed by the fans on the Kop. Although they were only kidding me, it did give me an insight into what it must be like to play against Liverpool at Anfield.

Later, when I became an England player and began to get involved in commercial contracts, Bobby Moore went out of his way to advise me. When you have admired and respected someone from a distance for a long time you always fear that you might be disappointed when you actually meet them. This was not my experience with Moore. I first met him when spending a weekend at the Toy Fair in Brighton, promoting Mettoy footballs. He took me to one side and said, 'You're going to get a lot of contracts and you're going to get a lot of "friends", hangers-on who want to know you because you're Kevin Keegan, just like I did because I was Bobby Moore. You've got to be in a position to handle these things and also business matters.'

He told me about his business affairs and how things had gone wrong for him. 'My night-club with Sean Connery,' he said, 'sounds great, but I've lost a fortune on it. I've also invested in other businesses and lost money. The only thing I've made money on is my little sports shop outside West Ham's ground.' This underlined the point that however much of a star you may be, you will fail unless you are handled right. In a roundabout way he told me not to go into business until I had finished playing football in case I was taken advantage of. It was the best advice I have had from any footballer, because it was from Bobby Moore, who had been through it himself. He need not have said anything to me. He could have thought, 'Here's a new star, let him find out for himself.' Instead, a man who had achieved the greatest honour in the game found time to put right a lad who was still learning what it was all about.

The Mettoy contract was my first really solid business deal with an established firm. Initially, I sat on the fence, refusing offers from smaller firms in order to get a contract to have my name on a good ball, and was fortunate to end up at the best company in Britain. I try to work this way, because I believe it is important what I put my name to. My name is everything I have got. If it became unpopular, either because I was playing badly on the field or getting adverse publicity, I have lost everything, because my name is my earning power.

9

Good, bad and Uglies

I was very much a stranger to Liverpool when I met Vic Huglin. We struck up a conversation in a club and he asked me what I thought of the city. 'The people are great, but I don't like it much as a place,' I told him. 'There are some nice parts,' said Vic, 'I'll show you around.' He took me out for a meal and we became close friends. Vic introduced me to the Liverpool I had not known. He and his family were very good to me.

Vic was the boss of a carpet warehouse and he became my first business agent. Within a week of kicking a ball for the first time for Liverpool, I was besieged by just about every agent in Great Britain, all promising me the earth. They scared me, because not all of them could have been sincere. I had distinct reservations about them, which explains why I was happy when Vic offered to handle my affairs. This was an ideal start for me. Not being an agent by profession, Vic was pleasant in the way he approached the job. He did very well and built me a good image, allowing me to sit on the fence for a year and assess who was really genuine in the world of big-time agents.

I was prepared to do a great deal of work for a small return during that formative year, because I realized that the main aim was to make a name for myself, with the public and with people in business. Vic worked hard for me as a sideline, but I do not think he ever understood what he was starting. Before long I was in great demand. Everybody has a limit, and I felt that Vic had reached his. I joined Paul Ziff at 'Public Eye', in Leeds, but Vic was written into the contract because he had set the wheels in motion. Later, Harry Swales took over my affairs.

During my early days at Liverpool I would occasionally go to night-clubs, which I found to be lonely places filled with people who were trying to create a false world for themselves. The lighting would be subdued and people would drink and talk out of character, as an escape from the normality of their everyday lives. It was almost as if they were actors and actresses, wearing masks and changing their personalities to suit the surroundings.

One night, Vic and I were talking together in a club called 'Uglies' when a girl came over and said to Vic, 'Your Mate is a right ...' The way she swore startled me. I hate to hear a girl swear, and she could have found another word to express her feelings without degrading herself.

'Which mate is that?' asked Vic.

'Kevin Keegan,' said the girl. She was looking at me as she talked to Vic, but obviously did not know who I was.

'Why, what's he done?' said Vic, giving me a puzzled look, as if to suggest that she was a crank.

The girl spared no details: 'He took me home on Christmas Eve and stayed with me all night – the usual thing – promising to come back the next afternoon with perfume and that. Typical footballer, he never turned up.' Some fellow had told the girl he was me and had slept with her. Now she was calling me all the names under the sun.

Vic interrupted her, 'I think I'd better introduce you to Kevin. . . .'

'Why, is he in here?' she said, glancing around.

'This is Kevin,' said Vic.

'That's not him,' she replied.

'That's Kevin Keegan,' Vic insisted.

She looked at me and said, 'You're not, are you?' The question made me feel strange, as if I were about to tell a lie.

'Well,' I said, 'I'm almost sure I am.'

After that incident I was not surprised how stories about me would travel around town. I have heard people say, 'I saw Kevin Keegan with a pint of beer in his hand last night,' and to improve upon this, someone else would say, 'When I saw him he was blind drunk.' That sort of thing starts when someone sees you having half-a-pint of lager in a club. He tells his friend he saw you with a pint, this friend tells another friend it was two pints, the next friend is told it was four pints, and the story ends with you rolling about, unable to stand.

I learned to live with this type of exaggeration. Jean has received letters telling her all kinds of tales. One was accompanied by a picture of a nude girl from *Playboy* magazine, and carried the message, 'I think you should see the standard of slag that your fellow is staying with when he goes down to London.' I had to laugh, even though this can be embarrassing and make you feel guilty without having cause to be. It is reassuring to know that Jean and I loved each other before I really got anywhere. If I met her now instead of then I doubt if we would feel the same way about each other or have the same trust. We are fortunate because, as we say in Yorkshire, Jean knew me when I had 'nowt'.

Jean always insists that I wanted to become engaged at Christmas 1971, although I cannot recall having said that! As it happened, events were virtually worked out for us when her parents had an opportunity to sell their fish and chip shop and move into the hotel business in Newquay. We talked matters over and it became clear that if Jean moved to Newquay with her parents, we would see so little of each other that the situation would become impossible. The only alternative was for Jean to take a job in Liverpool as soon as she finished her school examinations. We became engaged on Jean's eighteenth birthday, during the summer of 1972, when she also moved to Liverpool and went into digs with Mr and Mrs Roberts, or Gav and Lil as we know them with great affection. They were like second parents to Jean, and their daughter, Gill, is like a sister to us. Mrs Roberts was 'Fag Ash Lil' until she lost the nickname by giving up smoking.

Jean spent a year as an optician's receptionist, but she found the work lonely and became depressed because her parents were so far away. I attempted to snap her out of it by saying, 'You've got to become independent. You've got to go out on your own.' I thought it might help if I taught her to drive. After a few lessons, she became interested enough to have professional tuition – from a woman, in fact – and passed her test first time. I bought her a soft-topped MG Midget. It was an 'old banger', but Jean thought the world of it. The car also helped when she changed jobs and joined the Civil Service, as an assistant collector with the Income Tax department at Bootle. The job was rather monotonous but she made many friends. She also began to take cookery lessons 'for brides to be' on Wednesday evenings.

As Jean is the first to admit, she was very jealous and possessive during those early days in Liverpool. On one occasion, when Phil Niles came over to see a match, he and Jean were waiting for me in my car outside the ground. Just as I was about to climb in, a girl put her arms around my neck and gave me a great big kiss. This sort of thing happened all the time, and there was very little I could do about it. I do not like to brush people aside. Jean was so upset that she refused to speak to me all the way home. Her attitude then proved that she was still too young to get married, but gradually she became more independent and grew out of those fits of jealousy. We laugh about them now.

On another occasion, I made a record called 'It Ain't Easy', backed by the Fourmost pop group from Liverpool. I was rather dubious, because I am no singer, but I could not resist the chance of working in a recording studio in London, which had been used by the Beatles and other top stars. The lyrics were aimed at my way of life:

> It ain't easy, it ain't easy,
> It ain't easy to live this life with me,
> Believe me, it ain't easy,
> Cheering crowds in far off places,
> Lots of money in my hand,
> But I come home too tired for loving,
> Something a girl would find so hard to
> understand....

I had rehearsed the 'A' side, but the 'B' side, 'Do I Know You', was still being written right up to the time when Jean and I arrived at the studio. When they put the song in front of us, Jean looked at it and said, 'You're not singing this, Kev. It's not you.' It was about my sleeping with a girl whose name I did not know. If Jean had not been there, I might have gone through with it, but she was right. I have never looked for that kind of image and I never will. 'You can change that,' Jean told the writers, and the 'B' side was rewritten at the last minute. 'It Ain't Easy' did very well – we are still looking for the person who bought the third copy! In fact, the sales figures were around 12,000 and the record reached number seven in the Merseyside charts. Many people wrote saying they could not get hold of a copy and I wrote back saying how lucky they were.

Letters from football followers all over the world began to pile up, and Jean helped me organize a fan club. We made an office out of the back room of a junk shop in

Liverpool on song.

Golden boot : a souvenir of Wembley 1974.

Prescot Road. This was no ordinary junk shop. It was the land of 'Lennie the Junk', Lennie Libson, the best friend I will ever have outside football. I was introduced to him by Ray Clemence, who had wandered into the shop looking for records when he was in digs at Mrs Lindholme's. Lennie has a heart of gold. He is the type of person who likes doing favours, and has done so many good turns for me that I would not even be able to repay him if I started now and continued for the rest of my life.

After I had finished morning training I would frequently go to Lennie's. He had everything imaginable in the shop, and I loved to hear him bargaining with people. A poor woman brought in an old kitchen sink with a crack in it, but he gave the woman a pound, even though he knew that he would have to throw the sink away.

There was an old bicycle in the shop, with both wheels buckled and not a spoke to be seen, which Lennie had marked up for a pound. 'You're not going to try and sell that are you?' I asked. 'People have to pay to have things like that taken away!'

I used to shoot at targets with air pistols, which Lennie had an abundance of. When Alan Waddle moved into my digs after joining Liverpool from Halifax he would play Lennie's guitars. I even discovered Lennie wore a wig one day when he walked under a shelf packed with electric fires. The metal leg of a fire unit caught his head and his hair turned round! Sometimes I would serve the customers or sweep up and tidy the stock. It does not look nearly as neat now as when I was around. The only trouble was, after I had finished, Lennie could never find anything.

I cleaned out the back room and Jean and I decorated it, converting it into a cosy little office. We used it for the fan club and also as a base for my limited company, Nageek Enterprises (Keegan spelt backwards). I took this measure when the first contracts were put in front of me and I realized I was paying far too much tax. I decided to plan for the future, which meant taking a keen interest in my business affairs. I learnt about contracts and could rewrite one myself now because I know what to look for. When a firm makes an approach with a contract it is usually slanted in their favour, but a contract is an agreement between two or more parties, and I always ensure that it is also beneficial to me.

Liverpool is full of characters, but they are not all as nice to know as Lennie. There are the car thieves, for instance. My Cortina became a Liverpool taxi, and I would often catch sight of it as I drove around the city. The Capri became a jinx. Everything seemed to happen to that car. The first thing experience taught me when I came to Liverpool was to lock everything. In Doncaster, I could leave my car door open with all my belongings in the car and nothing would disappear. Thefts took place, of course, but in relatively small numbers compared with Liverpool. It is not extraordinary for a man to park his car in Liverpool and return to find it standing on bricks instead of wheels.

The Liverpool players would park their cars at the Crest Motel before leaving by coach for an away match. It was after a defeat at Derby – which was bad enough in itself – that I returned to find my car had gone. I reported its disappearance to the police and borrowed a car from a friend for a couple of days. The police later telephoned me to report that it had been found in Egypt Street, a rough area near the old Cathedral. Someone had taken the car from the Crest Motel, bumped it, pulled off the wing mirrors

My office, at the back of Lennie's junk shop.

and the rear mirror, ripped out the cassette player and smeared fish and chips all over the seats.

That was enough for me. I was extremely careful after that, but Liverpool is noted for ingenuity and novelty. When I parked the car outside my digs in Lilley Road, as an extra precaution, I bought a Krooklok. One morning, I climbed into the car and found everything in its place – except the Krooklok. Someone had actually stolen that and left everything else. I could only assume it was a joke. Where there is poverty, there will be stealing. If I were poor and had children who were starving, I would steal food for them. But in Liverpool, stealing is an industry organized by full-time professionals.

One night, I came out of 'Uglies' and discovered that my car was blocked by an E Type Jaguar and a Fiat. I went back to the club to ask if someone could announce the numbers and get the owners to let me out. A young man came to the door and asked what the trouble was. I told him I was jammed in, and there was no sign of the owners of the offending cars. He walked over to the E Type, took a piece of wire from his pocket, picked the lock, released the handbrake and pushed the car backwards. A bubble car prevented him from pushing the E Type right out of the path of my Capri, but he was able to use the wire to also pick this car's lock. There was still the Fiat to be tackled, which I thought he might have some difficulty with, but he had the door open in a flash. I drove away, believing he could have opened Fort Knox with that piece of wire.

There is an ailment peculiar to Liverpool called 'Kemlyn Road Knee', the sufferers being patrons of Anfield's Kemlyn Road Stand in which the seats are packed painfully close to each other. No doubt, it was a fan from the Kop who diagnosed Kemlyn Road Knee, because the Kopites diagnose just about everything. They are the funniest, noisiest, most famous fans in football. They shout themselves hoarse encouraging Liverpool and, although they respect good football and class players, they still do their best to unsettle opposing teams. 'Pinocchio! Pinocchio!' was their greeting to Mike Summerbee, with due respect to his nose. Summerbee's Manchester City team-mate, Franny Lee, would be treated to a chorus of 'Franny is a Womble.'

I had played only a couple of games for Liverpool when a supporter presented me with a red and white paper crown, but I was never 'King of the Kop'. The 'King of the Kop' was Bill Shankly. Nowhere else in the world would fans chant the manager's name before they chanted the names of the players. Shanks was like a player, doing everything except kick the ball into the back of the net for us. No manager ever had the kind of relationship with a crowd that Shanks had. He identified with them and they identified with him. They loved him because he had started with nothing, had worked his way up and built a club of which they could be proud.

The respect between Shanks and the fans made him more important to them than any single player. They prided themselves on their record of good behaviour at a time when hooliganism was rife in English football. They did not want to let Shanks down. I have seen troublemakers taken to one side and given a good hiding by lads from the Kop. This kind of rough justice was likely to take place anywhere; in a football ground, a town centre or on a train. If a lad behaved in a way that was likely to tarnish their reputation, they would sort him out. First they would try reasoning with him, but if that failed, someone would give him a belt. He would then know not to cause trouble again. This proved to be more effective than any action taken by a policeman.

Some of the followers of Manchester United established a reputation for hooliganism, became proud of it and lived up to it. That is a shame, because the majority of United fans are good supporters who want to encourage their team and see a good game of football. Many English fans can see no further than their own club. They will not accept that other clubs might have better players. A Birmingham fan said to me, 'You're not a bad player, but you're not fit to clean Trevor Francis's boots,' and at Leeds I was told, 'When you're as good as Tony Currie, you'll be getting somewhere.' Crowds never discourage me, no matter what they shout. I have played some of my best games away from home, when people have chanted 'Keegan wants his mammy' and 'Kevin Keegan, superstar, walks like a woman and wears a bra.' If anything, that gives me an even greater incentive to do well.

I sometimes wonder whether the Liverpool supporters have been spoilt by years of success. I do not wish to criticize them in any way or to be unfair, but I have a feeling that if the team had a bad run the club would lose 15,000 spectators. In my view, Liverpool have about 30,000 loyal supporters and 15,000 who have just followed the club's success. I am sure people on the Kop will agree that some Liverpool supporters are hard to please. Anything less than success just will not do for them, and one day these 15,000 could make life hard for the players in the first Liverpool team that really flops. I hope I am proved wrong and appreciate how fortunate I was to have had the fans on my side from the first day I wore a red jersey. They used to sing 'Kevin Keegan walks on water', but there were times when I felt as if I were walking on air.

As a schoolboy I had won a medal playing Doncaster junior league football, and as a professional I received a silver nut dish, roughly the size of one of my hands, when Scunthorpe were runners-up in the Lincolnshire Senior Cup. By the end of the 1972–73 season I had a League Championship medal, a UEFA Cup Winners' medal and assorted personal awards, to place alongside the junior medal and nut dish, displayed in a cabinet at my parents' home. Liverpool won the Championship with sixty points, three more than Arsenal and six more than Leeds United, and brought home their first trophy from Europe after years of striving. In the UEFA Final we beat the West Germans, Borussia Mönchengladbach, 3–2 on aggregate, winning the home leg 3–0 and holding on as the Germans attacked furiously in the return match. Two of the Borussia players, Gunther Netzer and Henning Jensen, later moved on to Real Madrid.

The winning of a trophy represents so much effort, yet it comes and goes in a flash. You receive the acclaim, then the cricket season starts and you are left with the approach of a new campaign in which to live up to the standards you have set. An FA Cup Final is special because you can savour every moment of it, but I could not single out any particular match that won the League Championship for us. The only way a team wins the League is by consistency. The UEFA Cup Final, played over two matches, home and away, was amazing in its contrast. We outplayed Borussia at Anfield and they outplayed us in Germany. It was not until some time after that it really sunk in that we had won.

I was bitterly disappointed with the financial return from winning the Double. We

Steve Heighway makes a break.

Ray Clemence, my team mate with Scunthorpe, Liverpool and England.

Olé!

slogged through a season, were successful at home and abroad, and the club gave us a bonus of only £2000 each, dwindling to little more than £400 after tax. Then came surtax demands from the previous year. What hurt most, and was especially depressing, was that people assumed we had earned a fortune. But I was learning to accept the drawbacks of what was, overall, a wonderful new life.

10

Lessons from Bestie

Without knowing it, George Best helped me considerably. As players, we are totally different, though it was inevitable that people would draw comparisons between us. I was a new 'name' and, like Bestie, I wore my hair long and played as a forward. Bestie, however, has more talent than I have. If I could achieve what he has as a standard of personal performance, I would finish my career knowing that I had achieved everything. I have too much respect for Best's play to criticize him. I attempted to copy him in some ways – every player would like to play the way Bestie does – and, apart from his more obvious skills, I was always impressed by the dedicated way he ran back to help his defence.

If there is one aspect of play in which I am superior to Bestie, it is in being a better team man. Bestie is a worker, but I think of football in terms of a team and feel that I fit into the framework of a team better than he does. Towards the end of his career with Manchester United, people began to talk about George Best and Manchester United rather than Manchester United with George Best. Before I attempt to analyse my game, let me make it clear that Bestie helped me most as an example of what could happen to a player caught up in adulation and business off the field of play. As soon as I was in demand to attend functions and endorse products, I set out to conduct myself differently from Bestie. I tried to learn from his mistakes. If I said I would go somewhere, then I went. I was determined not to let people down.

It was at the end of my second season at Liverpool that I got to know George Best, and the image of him presented to the public was not the one that came through to me. He had already experienced major problems at Manchester United, when we happened to be on the same plane to Majorca. We sat together but did not talk very much. Bestie is not a great conversationalist, though he has a good sense of humour. He seemed to be a little shy, which surprised me. I had expected to meet a flamboyant character to match the image. I had read so many things about him, some of which were no doubt true, but it was hard to believe that this was the same Bestie.

I saw him occasionally during the holiday. We played table-tennis and had drinks together. He struck me as being a nice guy, happy to take a back seat in the company of a group of people, listening more often than talking. Bestie had more hangers-on than most, yet he seemed to be a loner. He appeared to be confused, with nobody to depend upon. I felt sorry for him then, and I still do now. Later, when we knew each other better and I had experienced some of the problems he had, we talked more, though never at great length. Perhaps what Bestie did not realize was that if you begin doing things that attract publicity, such as being photographed with beautiful girls, you cannot just turn it off when it suits you. Football is like a one-way street. You pick your street and have to go right to the end of it before you can take another turning. There is no going back when half-way down a one-way street.

It begins in a small way. When something about you is going to be in the papers, you cannot wait to see it. Once your name is in the papers, you are playing well and people are talking about you, then you can consider yourself successful. Everybody should want to be successful. If you want to have your name on footballs and splashed across the papers, or if you want to appear on television, you have to accept all that goes with being in the public eye. If your picture is constantly appearing in the papers, you must expect to be recognized and sought after. I would love to go to the cinema without having everybody staring at me, elbowing each other and saying, 'It's Kevin Keegan', so that everyone else can hear. You have just got to pretend not to hear them. When I go to a restaurant for a meal, it would be pleasant to eat without feeling like a goldfish in a bowl. I used to love doing Christmas shopping, but now I just park my car outside a shop and rush in and out again to avoid a fuss.

Fame takes you from one extreme to the other. When I went home to Doncaster I had the feeling that some of my friends were apprehensive about approaching me. If they did, and I offered to buy them a drink, I wondered if they thought that I was flashing my money around. If I had not offered, they might have thought I was becoming tight-fisted. There are two sides to everything, and I can only examine the situation from my standpoint, but I think some of my old friends changed their attitude towards me more than I changed mine towards them. I became vulnerable, not knowing what to say or do when I met someone I had known in the past. I have said 'hello' to people who have not replied because they have been too shocked to hear me greet them, and this made me feel foolish.

Nothing has changed as far as my good friends back home are concerned. Whenever I see them, we still have a good night out together. Some people will say I have changed, and I suppose in some ways I have, but I do not believe my character is any different. I still have the same outlook on life. While some of the people I knew became reluctant to approach me, total strangers began to greet me like old friends. Initially, I was only recognized on Merseyside, where people would either smile and say 'hello', or have a joke at my expense, depending on whether they supported Liverpool or Everton. After a couple of seasons and a few appearances on television and in advertisements, people seemed to know me wherever I went. People who were not even interested in football would look at me as if they felt they should know me although they could not place me. This could be embarrassing. I would try to look the other way when it was obvious they could not figure out who I was. 'Are you who I think you are?' they would ask. 'No, but I wish I had his money,' I would joke.

Autograph hunters vary considerably. I have been followed miles from Oxford Street in London by someone who eventually caught up with me and said, 'I'm sorry to trouble you, but I didn't want to stop you in the main street. Would you sign this for me, please?' Other people have treated me like dirt: 'Hey! Sign this!' If that type of request comes from an adult, I put it down to ignorance, but when a child asks that way, I try to work on him or her.

'Sign that!'

'Sign that what?' I ask.

'Sign that, with a pen.'

'Sign that *what*?'

'Sign that piece of paper.'

I have spent two minutes with a kid before he has said 'please'. I do not want to make fools of them, but I expect a 'please' or a 'thank you' because I have been brought up that way.

I enjoy sharing a joke with people or exchanging banter, but, like everyone else, I have my off days. There are times when I would like to hide, but I realize that being in the public spotlight is part of the life I have chosen. Football has given me everything, and I appreciate that lack of privacy is one of the prices I have to pay. But I do agree with Bestie when he says that in America they build a superstar to worship him, while in England they build a superstar to knock him down. Bestie felt the full force of that himself. I know I might also experience it one day, when people decide they have had enough of me.

I do not think Michael Parkinson's 'Intimate Biography' helped Bestie. Doubtless, much of what was written was true, and Bestie felt a need to say what he did, but what did they hope to achieve by it? It would be nice to think you can fight everything, but you cannot. It takes a brave man to try – I respect that – but you cannot criticize everything and everybody and expect society to accept it. Bestie might have been in a better position if he had done what I did and made a move abroad when he was still a top-class player. I think he remained too long at one club and became stale. By the time he went to America, he had already experienced many problems and was almost thirty. My move was not made for the same reason. I have not had Bestie's troubles off the field, and Liverpool Football Club have not suffered, but I do need a change from English football.

Apart from his car crash, Bestie has been enjoying life and playing well again for Fulham. This pleased me, because, in spite of everything, I feel that Bestie has had a rough deal. I know he caused many of his own problems, but it was still a pity that everything went wrong for such a gifted player. I would like to see him in the First Division again, because it is harder to play in the Second Division. From experience, I would say that the higher the division, the easier it is for a player with ability. Within a few months of leaving the Fourth Division people were raving about me. No one can convince me that I had become a better player in so short a time. I was playing the way I had played before, but with better players and in front of a crowd which generated a marvellous atmosphere. To a certain extent, opposing players were laying off me and giving me more·time in which to make my moves.

I suppose I do understand how Bestie feels partly, but I do not know how he felt when the pressure was at its most brutal. Brutal might seem a bad choice of word, because, as I am the first to admit, it is nice to be popular, but, when people turned on Bestie and started to pull him down it must have been brutal for him. I am fortunate to have people to lean on, such as Jean and other good friends.

It has been said that Bestie might have been better off if he had gone to London sooner and escaped the suffocating effect of being the most famous person in Manchester. That is fair comment, but not necessarily right. Surely he would prefer to be playing for Manchester United, Liverpool, Leeds United or one of the other top clubs. With due respect to Arsenal, Spurs, West Ham, Queen's Park Rangers and the rest, there is no team to play for in London now where it is possible to be at the top of one's profession.

I enjoy the things that go with football, but my order of priority has always been football first, enjoyment second. I sometimes get the impression that certain players think the other way round; the social life is all important, and football is only necessary in order to maintain it. Fear is the element that ensures most players' dedication. If I lived in London and my club was coasting towards the League Championship, I just might be tempted to go out on one or two Thursday nights. When you are young it is much more enjoyable to go to a night-club and have a good time than it is to stay in, watch television and go to bed early, with the next match in mind. It could be argued that if I did go out and was recognized, it would not matter because London is a big city and has such a glamorous reputation that people are used to seeing celebrities. I would not have dreamed of going out at night after Wednesday when I was playing for Liverpool. Somebody would have seen me and word would somehow have got back to the boss. On the occasions at Liverpool when the lads did go out and have a good time, we would joke, 'When you think about it, this football is interfering with our social life.' But we would never forget what we owed to football. Had it not been for football, no one would have wanted us to advertise their goods, open their shops, present their prizes or play in their pro–am golf tournaments.

Bestie was a great footballer but still found time to do the things he wanted to do, and I admire him for that. If he was able to do them both successfully – as he did for a long time – good luck to him, but I think eventually it caught up with him. A footballer's career is so fleeting that he has to keep things in perspective all the time. He has to always remember who he is and what he is.

My game is completely centred on my work rate. I get involved for the full ninety minutes and receive the ball so much because I have an appetite for it. I do not look upon myself as a skilful player and never have done, no matter how much people have tried to convince me that I am. I know that I have a degree of skill. I know what I can and cannot do, but if people use the expression 'world class' when they talk about me, I hope they do so because I know how to bring out the best in the players around me and, therefore, make a better player of myself.

If someone gave me a ball and asked me to do some tricks with it, I would not be interested. I have never practised circus tricks. When I was a boy, I could keep the ball in the air with my feet for as long as I chose to, but I spent most of my time concentrating on the skills which would matter most in an actual game. I would use the wall at the bottom of my garden to sharpen up my timing and my heading and shooting abilities. Occasionally in training I will take a ball and juggle with it for a short time, but only to get the feel of it. I am not interested if a player can keep a ball in the air forever. When people have said to me, 'We've got a great young lad in our team, who can keep the ball up for a thousand kicks,' I have told them to find the boy a circus. I am only interested when people say, 'We've got a great young lad who works hard, scores goals and makes goals,' because those are the things that the game is about.

I think it is a sin and a shame that Rodney Marsh and Stan Bowles waste their skills by just drifting in and out of a game as and when they feel like it. A player's true potential can never be realized if he adopts that attitude towards his play. I have heard the argument that a skilful player should not have to do the running and the chasing, which can be left to the less gifted players in a team. But if a player is prepared to run and work, he will become more involved in the game and get a better response from the people around him. My strength is that people know that if I am having a bad game it is not because I want to but just because things are not working out. When things are going badly, I will try twice as hard.

The reason why I am respected by many people in England is not because they can recall any brilliant games I might have had, but because they have seen me play perhaps forty-six times in a year without me having what could be termed a nightmare or a 'stinker'. I am self-critical, but I can think of only half-a-dozen games after which I have walked off the pitch and said to myself, 'Well, sunshine, you were diabolical.' My work on the pitch has always been directed towards achievement. I do not play fancy tricks with the ball, just to impress people. I have tried to give my energy and what skill I have to the team, to help them to win trophies. The reason why Liverpool have been so successful is that one or two individual players have knitted into the general pattern of the team.

Much has been said and written about my partnership with John Toshack. We were even put through a mental telepathy test on television, although the result was negative. That was not surprising, because Tosh and I are not even great friends off the field. We have never been really close, but I do like him. I even find his occasional cockiness endearing. A typical Tosh comment was made when he returned after injury and said, 'When I went out of the side we were on top of the League and when I came back I put us back on top of the League.'

Tosh can be a strange mixture. Sometimes he thinks he is a better player than he is, and on other occasions he will not give himself enough credit. Opponents have often been guilty of underrating Tosh. They have taken steps to curb his ability in the air, while neglecting to watch him closely with the ball at his feet – and Tosh puts a chance away better than any other big man I have seen. We got on so well together on the field because we both thought deeply about our game. We knew each other's strengths and weaknesses – playing to our strengths while trying to hide our weaknesses. I could have made Tosh look a fool and he could have done the same to me, but that is not the idea of the game. We have had our ups and downs and kidded each other, but when it came to serious talk I always found Tosh willing to listen to advice. I think he would say the same about me.

Our success together was due more to the thought that went into it than to the physical side. I am sure we thought more about our play than any other partnership has. We always took it for granted that opposing teams had been watching us and had planned ways of making us less effective. We were likely to talk things over at any time and in any place. It might have been five minutes before we left the dressing-room or during the kick-about before the match. Sometimes, it was even during the game. In an effort to be one move ahead of the opposition we would attempt to work out what they expected us to do. We then did the opposite. For instance, I might say to Tosh, 'They're expecting me to run to the near post when the ball comes across, so you go there every time, and I'll go to the far post.' Someone else might have watched that game and consequently we would revert to our old style for the next match.

We might go into a match with a special move at the back of our minds but no definite plan to implement it and, on the spur of the moment, one of us would say, 'Remember what we said? Let's try it!' On some occasions Tosh would not be having any success against the big defenders, and I would offer to take them on. That might sound stupid, but it worked. Eventually our play was almost instinctive, although there was the occasional period when we lost communication. During a match against Manchester United, I moved into a good scoring position, unmarked, but instead of laying the ball back to me Tosh tried a shot from a ridiculous angle and a great chance was missed. 'You greedy big bastard,' I said. 'That's the last time I help you out. Don't you ever speak to me again!' I refused to talk to him at half-time, but within five minutes of the second half I broke clear with the ball down the left and spotted Tosh in the middle on his own. There was a strong temptation to try a shot, just for spite, but the game is bigger than that sort of pettiness and I laid the ball to Tosh, who knocked it into the net. He came over and congratulated me. 'Yes,' I said, 'and if you'd done that in the first half we wouldn't have had an argument and the game would have been sewn up.' As a result of what I said, Tosh spent the next twenty-five minutes trying to lay a goal on for me. There was one instance when I was out on the wing and Tosh was in the middle. The ball was at his feet and the goal was at his mercy, but instead of having a shot, he pushed the ball across to me, even though I did not have a hope of scoring.

It would be wrong to say I will not miss Tosh. Many people have said to me, 'Tosh won't survive without you, but you'll survive without him.' I am sure we will both survive, although I may have a few more alternatives in my game. Liverpool will have to find someone else, similar to me, to buzz around Tosh and get the best out of him. I prefer to play off a big fellow like Tosh, but if there is not one in the team I can then become a target man myself or play in midfield. When Liverpool signed Ray Kennedy from Arsenal and Tosh was left out of the side for a while, I had to start learning the basics of playing alongside a new partner. Ray and I were beginning to work quite well together until he was moved into midfield. We could have been a good partnership, although I do not know whether we would have reached the same standard as Tosh and myself. I would never attempt to take any credit away from Tosh. I have had more than my fair share of the praise at Liverpool, not as a result of actively seeking it, but the big man was superb to play alongside.

During my last season at Liverpool my game began to alter somewhat. I still worked hard, but I began to look for something different. I dreaded the thought that 'something

a)

b)

c)

d)

e)

a) Tosh plays decoy and lets the ball drop for me.

b) It's under control..

c) A dribble past Leeds goalkeeper David Stewart.

d) The ball's on its way . . .

e) Into the net!

different' might be the temptation to play like Rodney Marsh and become more of a showman. People had analysed my game and become content just to stop me, even if it took two men – one for a position and one for a space. Teams would place an extra man in the areas where I used to run, and the additional cover meant that I was winning fewer balls in the air. But my game has time to develop and I hope the move abroad will give me the impetus I need.

Everyone's game can be improved, and I am no exception. To begin with, I know that my finishing should be better. I should score more goals, which means becoming a little more selfish. That frightens me, because I do not want to be selfish. I have always had as big a thrill out of laying on a goal as I have of scoring one myself. I have been criticized for this.

Malcolm Macdonald, who is a good friend, was once quoted in a newspaper article as saying that if he were a manager he would fine me every time I moved into my own half of the field. Malcolm is the type who can score almost thirty goals every season and have nothing to show for it, whereas I like to be able to look at my medals occasionally. All Malcolm thinks about is scoring goals, whereas my attitude is different. Much of my game is played outside the penalty box, where I might make a goal for someone else. Perhaps I will change, but at Liverpool I would rather have scored one and let Tosh score one than have scored two myself. It did not matter to me as long as the result was right and my form was consistent.

When my consistency has been broken, it has either been because of the general frustration of the team or because of something not connected with football at all. Perhaps Dad had been ill or I had carried a family worry on to the pitch with me.

I can put most problems out of my mind during a game. I often feel almost relieved to get on to the field. Much has been made of the pressures and tension in the game, but most of this lies on the outskirts of the game itself. When the whistle goes I am as free as I will ever be. No worries about tickets. No one is going to stop me for an autograph while I am running along the wing. People can shout abuse, but I rarely hear it. I am fortunate enough to know that, all things being equal, when I go out to play a game I am going to enjoy it. I do not like being kicked or spat at. Neither do I like being provoked, being booked or being sent–off. All these things can happen, which makes the game interesting.

Although I have shared jokes with referees, I have also had strong words to say to them. I have Irish blood in me, and sometimes my temper rips, but when I have been sent off it has been because I have retaliated after being provoked beyond what any normal man would stand.

I can recall only one occasion when I hurt someone without the slightest provocation. It was when I took out my feelings over a family matter on the unsuspecting Norwich City defender, Duncan Forbes. The worst thing Dad could do was to say something to upset me immediately before a game. I was bound to sulk, become irritable and do something stupid. Dad upset me before the Norwich game, and I went out in a temper. Usually when I came after big Forbsie I would laugh at him and say, 'I wonder how many times I'll be picking myself up off the floor today?' But that day I had other things on my mind. After some twenty minutes, when the ball was in the air between

Forbsie and myself, something just snapped. Not bothering about the ball, I jumped up and butted Forbsie. 'That's for all the times you've kicked me!' I said. Forbsie was stunned in more ways than one. My head was throbbing and I thought the referee was going to send me off. After the game, Forbsie came down to the dressing-room with a big plaster on his head. 'What's eating you, wee man?' he said.

'Look, I'm sorry,' I replied lamely, finding it hard to explain why anyone would do anything so stupid, 'something just snapped in my head. ...' Forbsie knew that what I had done was completely out of character, and he was still wearing a puzzled look as he left the ground. Only now, reading this, will he know the reason why I went for him.

I pride myself that I care about people and I thought the world of my father. When I moved to Liverpool I still tried to see him once a week. I could always tell immediately if I had done something to upset him, and this would hurt me as well. He would nag me over something I felt was petty. Perhaps I had begun to talk to him when someone else had called me over. He would have resented the fact that I had left him, even for a few moments. Or perhaps I had not telephoned him on the Friday before a game when I had promised I would. I might have had a very good excuse but Dad would react before I had a chance to explain.

I cared so much for my parents that I wanted them to share in everything I had, but this is not as easy as it sounds. I decided to buy them a house for instance, thinking, 'Here's one chance I've got to repay them a little for all they've done for me.' When they moved in I felt worried because they had left the environment they were used to and I wondered if they would settle. They, in turn, were so proud that they were almost against the move, simply because they did not feel they should let me do it. It was a strange situation. I was trying to do what I thought was right, and yet I could also understand their point of view. They were worried that in a couple of years time I might not be playing football. But everything worked out well and Dad spent four marvellous years there.

One time when I went to visit them, Mum made a sarcastic remark about money. 'What's Mum saying?' I asked. 'You know what we're on about,' said Dad. They had read in a magazine that I was earning £60,000 a year, and thought that I must have that much and more in the bank. 'I wish I had!' I said, but they looked sceptical. I had to explain exactly what I was being paid, how much tax I was liable for and where the rest of my money was going. The magazine statement had been taken out of context. I had never been one for discussing all my business interests with them, or anybody else for that matter. If I had done, it would only have been an extra worry for them.

They knew they would never be impoverished as long as I could work. They would never be wealthy, either, because this was not what they wanted. We soon settled the matter of the £60,000. Only seeing me once a week, once a fortnight and sometimes only once every three weeks, my parents tended to follow any news of me in the papers, which could be dangerous, because it was not always completely accurate.

11

Alf, and a drop of scotch

Sir Alf Ramsey won the World Cup for England when I was a schoolboy and lost it in Mexico when I was a Fourth Division player. While I was making a name for myself at Liverpool, he was facing the new and difficult experience of having to force England through a qualifying group, with Wales and Poland as rivals for a place in the 1974 Finals in West Germany. Two days after my twenty-first birthday, in February 1972, Alf gave me my first England chance with an Under-23 place against Scotland at Derby. I can remember thinking, 'I've come a long way in a short time.' In fact, it proved to be a long time before I found my feet as an international player.

I did not play well in that game at Derby. Very few players did, because the Baseball Ground was in a terrible state at the time, the muddy pitch making it difficult for any player with speed or ball control to show his ability. Martin Buchan played for Scotland. It was shortly before his transfer from Aberdeen to Manchester United, and he did his usual quiet but efficient job. We drew 2–2 with Mickey Channon scoring both our goals.

The following month I was selected again, for an Under-23 international against East Germany at Ashton Gate, Bristol – where my old Doncaster hero, Alick Jeffrey, had broken a leg, also playing for the England Under-23 side. The East Germany game was another disappointment. We were beaten 1–0, which came as a shock because Alf appeared to have selected a strong, promising team.

I was delighted to keep my place for the close season tour of East Germany, Poland and Russia, but was sent-off against East Germany shortly after half-time for aiming a kick at their 'hatchet' man, Klaus Decker. He had been told to mark me, and Decker took the job literally, kicking me when I had the ball and kicking me again when the ball had gone and the referee was not looking. Finally, he whacked me when the ball was at the other end of the pitch, and I retaliated. The Russian linesman ran some thirty yards on to the pitch, pointed me out to the referee, and off I went. I had scored in the first half and we were leading 2–1 when I was sent off. After this the East Germans equalized, making me feel somewhat guilty. I had let Alf down by being sent off and similarly the other players by putting extra pressure on them. Fortunately, we went on to win 3–0 in Poland and held the Russians to a goalless draw. Alf was unable to attend the disciplinary hearing, but he sent a letter to the Football Association, stressing that Decker had provoked me, and the FA took no further action against me. That did not make what I had done right, but it was good to know Alf had supported me.

Under-23 appearances do not automatically lead a player to the senior international team, but Alf gave me that promotion – although I am still not convinced that he really wanted me. I may be wrong, but I do not think Alf rated me as a player at that time. I have a feeling that pressure from outside influenced his decision to call me into the squad and select me for the team. No doubt Alf would disagree but other people wanted me to play and he had reached a situation where he had to try something new. Don Revie has experienced similar pressure. The press have continually thrown players' names at him, some of them being quite unlikely – Derek Hales, even before he moved from Charlton to Derby, is a good example – but if they are plugged often enough they begin to appear feasible.

Alf gave me two chances, the World Cup matches against Wales, but though England picked up three points, I was hardly a sensation. In my early days I had known failure – failure to win a place in the Doncaster Boys' team and failure to be taken on by Coventry – and this was another setback. At the time people said, 'What's up with Ramsey? He doesn't let you play the way you do for Liverpool.' But Alf's instructions were, 'Play your natural club game.' Although I tried, I found that my inexperience did not allow me to play well without my Liverpool team mates. A forward is always under pressure. Your place is in jeopardy if you win 1–0, let alone if you can only manage a goalless draw – and those were our two results against Wales. Malcolm Macdonald scored five goals against Cyprus, which one thought would have guaranteed his place for about two years, but within two matches he was out of the side.

Alf put me alongside Rodney Marsh and Martin Chivers, and until a manager experiments with a new blend of players he cannot possibly know whether it will work. I just might have been able to bring something extra out of Marshie, and he done likewise for me, but it did not happen. Chivers might have been like Toshack to me, but he wasn't. At Liverpool, if I made a move into an inside position, Tosh would move out wide. But when I moved inside for England, both Marshie and Chivers stood still, leaving me nowhere. I ended up wandering out on to the wing, feeling frustated and disillusioned. 'If this is international football,' I thought, 'I can't wait to get back to Liverpool!'

Alf was criticized for not selecting me again, but, in fairness, it was a risk he could not repeat. He had tried me twice and I had flopped. He was intent on trying to qualify for the World Cup. In a way I felt like an intruder. The spirit of 1966 and 1970 was still around that squad, even though most of the old faces had gone. When a new face appears it means that an old face has disappeared. It also happens at club level. You have a successful side, but every time someone new arrives, one of your old friends goes – like Peter Cormack at Liverpool. Although you might not resent the newcomer, you cannot help thinking about your old colleague.

I felt there was an England clique, despite getting on well with most of the lads as individuals. There would be little digs now and again, such as 'Look at him – just arrived and already pouring the tea! Really getting jobs with responsibility!' There was nothing really nasty. I dislike very few players, although there are probably many who do not like me. There is always a chance of that happening. You have to take the rough with the smooth in a game like football. I remember Alan Ball being good fun, and Bobby Moore was eager to help and pass on his experience. Moore did not stay in a clique, neither was he a captain who would dive off to his room. He remained with the team

Duet with Colin Todd of Derby.

Up and away.

Nodding home past Coventry's Jim
Blyth.

and had a knack of smoothing things over if players hurt each other's feelings. He had an aura. He did not have to shout, but just whisper, and people would listen.

When England failed to qualify, people were quick to say that we should have won both games against Wales comfortably, as if Wales were an easier proposition than Poland. But at that time, before they impressed the world in West Germany, Poland were regarded as a second-rate football nation. I would rather have faced Poland four times than Wales twice and Poland twice.

It is always difficult to play against Wales, Scotland, Northern Ireland and the Republic of Ireland, because the players you come up against know your style of play better than any other players in the world. Most of them are in competition against you during the course of a League season, and some play alongside you in your club team. Tosh knows all about me and I know all about him. Tosh, in turn, knows all about Ray Clemence, and vice versa. When England played the Republic of Ireland recently, Steve Heighway was in an ideal position to pass on tips about us to them. It can be like chess. If there are two good players on opposing sides, who know each other's game, one will make a move, the other will counter it, and they may eventually cancel each other out. Even within the England squad, I have often thought it strange how players are given opportunities to study each other for future reference by practising penalty kicks – Gerry Francis against Ray Clemence, for instance. It might seem like a small point, but six months later Queen's Park Rangers could be playing Liverpool and Francis might have to take an important spot-kick against Clemence.

Alf always sounded a little posh to be a football manager – 'Most certainly we will attack the opposition' or 'Most certainly this is our strongest squad.' There was an air about him that suggested he might think himself a cut above the players. Nothing could be further from the truth. Alf was a great fellow for the players. You will not hear many players criticize him, not even those who feel they should have had more opportunities. Alf always picked players who he believed were capable of doing a job for him. How else could a player like Peter Storey have won so many caps? There were more skilful players than Storey to choose from. He is not my type of player at all. He often marked me when I played against Arsenal, and would try to stop me in any way he could, which he was good at. He was so cool about it. His approach to a game could be as cold as his eyes. I would not rate him in the same class as Norman Hunter, for instance, but Alf knew he could rely on Storey to do the same vital job that Nobby Stiles had done – winning the ball and giving it to a team mate. A point in Storey's favour was that he would always be quick to give the ball to someone he knew could do something with it. He knew his limitations.

Alf and I were never close. We did not really have time to get to know one another, but I found him fairly predictable. He rarely surprised people and if anyone annoyed him, he would dismiss them tactfully and without fuss. A manager has to lean towards his players, something the press do not seem to realize. If he gravitates towards the press at the expense of his players, he has no chance of success. Once he loses the goodwill of the players he has lost everything, because he is only as good as the players make him. Pressmen want to print stories before they happen. They want to know the team before the manager has had time to tell the players. Neither Alf nor Don

Revie would tolerate that. Alf was only concerned with his players. He was probably wrong to be quite so emphatic about this, but he did, at least, win the respect of the players.

During Alf's period as manager, England beat Scotland 1–0 at Wembley, Martin Peters scoring the goal late in the game with a header at the far post. I did not play, but I took Jean along to watch it and what an experience it turned out to be. As anyone who has been to one of those games will know, there are 90,000 Scotsmen in the crowd and 10,000 Englishmen who are frightened to shout for their team. This makes the England players feel as if all 100,000 people are against them. They might just as well be playing away from home.

A few places along our row was a fellow who reminded Jean of someone. It was Rod Stewart. There he was, standing on his seat, clapping his hands, shouting 'Scotland!' and acting the clown like the rest of them. Where football is concerned, Rod is as daft as some of the other Jocks. I don't mean daft in a nasty sense. The game affects them that way. They love their football.

When the match had finished, I took Jean's hand and said, 'Come on, we'll go and see the lads and say ta-ra to the boss and shoot off.'

We went along to the dressing-rooms, and the Jocks were pouring out of the ground. Odd ones recognized me and shouted abuse, but in a good-natured way.

'Come on, Jean,' I said. 'We'll take a short cut round the back of the coaches,' only to come upon the amazing sight of hundreds of Jocks relieving themselves at the back of caravans and hot dog stalls. I hurried Jean back towards the players' tunnel, and we climbed aboard the England team coach. Eventually, the players who were taking a lift arrived, including Moore and Ball, along with Alf and his wife. As the bus pulled away from the stadium Jean and I came across the funniest scene of our lives. There were thousands of Jocks. Some were clutching bottles and looked blotto. They were still shouting and waving, even though England had beaten them. Ballie sat at the front of the coach, forming a one and a nought with his fingers and gesturing to remind them of the score as we drove slowly along Wembley Way.

This made the Jocks even more mad, and they began to clout the coach with their bottles. It was a good job the windows were made of unbreakable glass. One fellow approached the window in front of Ballie's seat, thumped it with his fist and staggered away, doubling up with pain. His friends rushed forward to examine his hand. Others began to attack, hitting and kicking the coach, then hobbling away and falling on to the road. When we looked back, there was a trail of casualties. Some of them must have ended up with hands and feet in plaster, although that would not have deterred them. They save for a year to come to London and more than half of them never even see the match.

When Joe Mercer was caretaker manager of England, he left me out of a match at Hampden Park because he wanted to try a new formation. England lost 2–0 on that occasion, but again Jean and I were amongst the crowd. The Jocks recognized me and although I was verbally attacked they also made me feel welcome. When the whisky began to flow, they made sure that the bottle was passed over to Jean and me – 'Have a swig!' – and we took a drink to be polite. They are magical supporters, and I love them for that. I do not mind these fanatical supporters who will follow their team, win, lose or draw.

When Scotland play, it's like having 100,000 Bill Shanklys on their side. Without the whisky, of course!

12

Red Army ensemble

I have never taken drugs, but I would imagine that the nearest thing to a psychedelic experience must be winning the FA Cup Final at Wembley. When Liverpool beat Newcastle United 3–0 in the 1974 Final, I was consumed by the whole event. I felt as if I were in another world, watching Kevin Keegan score two goals.

That Cup Final made me. It pushed me an important step further towards the top of my profession at a time when I was seriously considering quitting football. Even the week before the Final I was thinking, 'If Liverpool win this, I'll have won most things, so why not try something else?' I love football, but the game itself is only a very small part of being a player and I had reached the point where I had begun to wonder if it was worth all the aggravation. In the space of three years I had been transformed from an obscure Fourth Division player into one of the top commercial prospects in the game.

Jean and I had spent a great deal of time looking around Cheshire and North Wales for a place to live when we were married, eventually buying a cottage at Cilcain, near Mold. I began working on it, with both my mind and my hands. Plans were made for extensions and renovations. Finally, I moved in on my own to supervise the progress, stage by stage, from gamekeeper's cottage to our new home.

While I worked, I considered my future. Football was not everything to me then, and never will be. I see my life in broader terms. I had done well enough, but wasn't there something else I could turn to for a change. Two things pushed that question to the back of my mind. One was the enthusiasm of the Cup Final and the other was commonsense. Although I kept trying to tell myself that I did not need football, I was restrained by the fear of discovering too late that perhaps I did. If I knew I could step into a job which would guarantee me the same security, I would think very seriously about it. I have often said to Jean and my family that although I enjoy the ninety minutes of a match, I hate some of the things that accompany it.

I detest searching out tickets for people, for instance. There was a man from Wrexham who used to help me up at the house. He started off wanting two tickets for the match, then it was three and later it became five. I liked the fellow, but I felt he was using me to a certain extent, perhaps without meaning to. I was putting pressure on myself. My ticket allocation was twelve, and if additional members of my family or friends came over I would have to grovel round for extras. When Liverpool played Everton, the ticket position was dreadful. I did not help myself by trying very hard not to disappoint people.

A goal against Stoke . . . and Alan Bloor is a picture of disappointment.

A goal against Dynamo Dresden.

The Cup Final brought a special problem. I forget how many tickets I was allocated, but there were not enough. There never is. My father wanted two more for members of the family. Naturally, relatives are keen to see one of their own play in a Cup Final, even though they show little or no interest in all the other games. For my parents' sake, I agreed to supply the tickets, but when I checked to see how many I had left, I realized I was in trouble. Someone would have to miss out on a stand seat. I had an old uncle, but I could not ask him to stand up at the match. What worried me sick was that I might be forced to disappoint a friend called Tommy Ryan, who worked at Vic Huglin's carpet warehouse.

Tommy was a Liverpool supporter, through and through, who attended every match. I always provided him with his stand ticket, for which he paid, but there would be no seat at Wembley for Tommy. I went to see him, hoping that he would not be too upset at having to take a couple of standing tickets. 'Tommy, I've got bad news for you,' I said, and his head dropped. 'I can't get you a seat. I've only got these two, for standing up.' His face lit up and he all but kissed me, saying, 'I thought for a minute you were going to tell me you hadn't got me a ticket. One will do.' 'No,' I said, 'take a mate.'

Tommy was thrilled just to be able to stand at Wembley. Like so many of the genuine football supporters, he did not take anything for granted. Lads like Tommy are the ones who really matter. Others refuse to accept that you cannot please everyone or that you might have other matters on your mind. One man actually stopped me just as I was about to walk out on to the field one time and said, 'Where's my tickets?' I had to ask a member of the staff to take some money out of my pocket and buy a ticket for his friend, who was still outside. I am sure that one day, I will be playing on the pitch, when someone will run on, tap me on the shoulder and say, 'You forgot my bloody tickets!'

After that Final, when I played at Wembley for England, I joked with the lads and told them, 'I'll show you where they put the plaque to celebrate my first goal.' On recollection, Liverpool were so confident it was frightening. There was no thought of even the slightest chance of losing, or of not playing well. We did not think we would win as easily as we did, of course. We could not possibly have known that Newcastle would play so badly. Before the match, we stayed at St Albans, and on the Friday night Bill Shankly and Joe Harvey, the Newcastle manager, were interviewed by David Coleman on BBC television. While Shanks was doing this live programme, we players were watching in the next room. Shanks was full of his usual quips, while Joe, who never looked confident but was normally a good talker on television, seemed a little tense. When Shanks thought the interview had come to an end he turned to the person next to him and said, 'Christ, Joe's a bag of nerves, he's beaten already!' That came over loud and clear and we doubled up laughing, but the incident might have been a good psychological blow for us. It must have gone through the minds of the Newcastle players that there was a stark contrast in the moods of the respective managers.

As our coach approached Wembley, everywhere was mass of either red and white or black and white. We did not need a pep talk. We had to beat Newcastle for those people in red and white. When we came off the coach we were greeted by cheers. Even the directors must have felt that they could play and win. We walked into the dressing-room, and I took a quick look to see that my boots were under number seven. Still in our suits, we then went out to sample the atmosphere, say a few more words for the television, and take a look at the pitch. 'They keep complaining about it, but I wish we played here every week,' someone said. The band was in full swing, and as we walked around we heard great cheers from the Liverpool end and boos and whistles from the Newcastle end. When Sunderland beat Leeds, the fans from the north-east chanted 'Haway the lads!' but on this occasion one of the banners at the Liverpool end gave Newcastle the message, 'No way, the lads!'

Back in the dressing-room, we exchanged a few jokes. Shanks walked around, as busily as ever, constantly barking out instructions. Joe Fagan massaged legs and said to each of us in turn, 'I wish I was playing here, son.' Before we knew it, there was a knock at the door and it was time to go. Shanks marched us out, shouting as usual. We could see that he, more than anyone, wanted to win. He was obviously proud of the lads and he knew he was on a winner. The television recording later confirmed what we had sensed at the time. As the teams walked out, Joe Harvey was drawn and pale. Shanks was waving at everybody. Bobby Moncur looked pensive. Emlyn Hughes looked as if he was enjoying himself. Typical 'Emma', with that big grin on his face. Behind him were the other Liverpool players, loose and free. Ever since that Final I have made a point of studying players' faces and attitudes as they walk out. Manchester United looked confident – perhaps over-confident. Southampton looked as if they had come to do a job. Newcastle looked a little afraid.

It was a supporter's final. There was almost constant chanting. You could not have asked for another atmosphere quite like that meeting of Liverpool and Newcastle, bringing together the two most vocal sets of supporters in the country. 'Supermac, superstar, how many goals have you scored so far?' Malcolm Macdonald had been boasting to the papers about what he was going to do to Liverpool. When will players learn? Boosting your side is one thing, but deprecating the opposition in public merely gives them extra incentive to do well. It saves their manager a job. Liverpool had played it quietly. We were confident we could win but that was all we had said.

Liverpool were so superior on the day that it was hard to believe that it was the Final of one of football's greatest competitions. Yet Newcastle returned to their dressing-room at half-time without a goal having been scored against them. Early in the second half, Alec Lindsay passed the ball to me, I passed it back to Alec and he lashed it into the far corner of the Newcastle net. Alec and I were jumping up and down and hugging each other near a corner flag, but then we turned round. Supermac had the ball out on the left wing at the other end of the pitch. I had been ruled offside and the goal was disallowed. I still get annoyed when I think about that decision. Alec's shot was unstoppable, so how could I have been interfering with play? I do wish referees would use their discretion more often.

Penalty awards can be another source of annoyance. I think they should only be given when a player is fouled and he is in a scoring postion. If the player is certain to score – for example, if he has beaten the goalkeeper and is then brought down – the Laws should be changed to enable referees to award a penalty goal, instead of putting that team through the ordeal of taking a spot-kick. If it is a case of a player being fouled in the penalty area during the build-up towards a shot at goal – a man in the corner of the box, trying to work himself into a good position, for instance – the referee should be able to award a free kick, or even a corner. He should deal with every offence justly, irrespective of where it occurs.

Looking back on matches. I always remember the bad things that happened as well as the moments that pleased me. The Cup Final was no exception. I recall having had a chance to score with a header early in the first half, but waited for the ball to come to me instead of moving for it beforehand. Alan Kennedy, showing confidence in spite of his inexperience, cleared the ball with a superb overhead kick. More important, there was my first goal, which should never have been a goal. With due respect to Iam McFaul, I do not think my shot would have beaten Ray Clemence. Some people thought it was a great goal but all they had seen was the ball hitting the top corner of the net. I was just inside the penalty area when the chance came, and though I put plenty of power behind the ball, the angle of my shot was not right. The ball was about a yard off the course I had intended it to take, and McFaul was able to get a full hand to it. He could only push it into the corner of the net, which was where I had intended to put it initially.

Steve Heighway scored a brilliant second goal, the second time he had scored in a Final. Not many players have achieved that. On this occasion, in contrast to 1971, his goal was part of a success story. The third goal, which I tapped over the line from the thirteenth pass of the move, delivered by Tommy Smith, typified Liverpool's display. It was a team goal and appropriate because everyone had played his part in the victory. We were as good as Newcastle were bad, which is why the match was so one-sided. It is fair to say that Liverpool have played better and lost, but the most significant and pleasing part of our performance against Newcastle was that millions of people saw it on television. People saw the other side of a team the critics called 'Shankly's Robots', 'Shankly's Machine' and 'Shankly's Red Army' – true communists, all work and no entertainment. We had worked and entertained.

When the final whistle went we were able to savour every moment of a result which we had richly earned. Before we went up to collect the Cup and our medals, we shook hands with the Newcastle lads. At that point I felt more sorry for them than elated for us. Winner takes all, and when I looked back at the faces of the Newcastle players, it was obvious that many of them now wished they had never got to Wembley. How could we console them? They had given one of the worst Wembley performances for years, but they did not want or expect pity. Shanks chatted with them, which was typical of him. Before a game he would pull the opposition apart by telling us they were useless, but afterwards he would make a complete retraction. He was once very critical about Bobby Moore, but after the game he announced, 'You've just played against the best player in England.'

We had won the Cup and it was then time to thank our supporters, because without them we would not have been at Wembley. Although I ought to have been tired, I felt quite refreshed as I jogged around the stadium, waving to the fans. I did not hold the cup – a couple of the players had their hands welded to it – but I was happy enough to see it being paraded in front of me. Three-quarters of the way round the track I felt that someone was missing, and realized that it was Bill Shankly. We had forgotten about the most important person, and he had walked off. Back in the dressing-room, Shanks acted as if a big weight had been lifted from his shoulders. I sensed that he was not quite his usual self, but did not give the matter much thought at the time.

When the team had returned, empty handed after the 1971 Final, the city of Liverpool turned out in force, but Jean and I left the train at Allerton and went home. We did not feel a part of what had happened. We were, however, very much a part of the 1974 homecoming, when some half-a-million people lined the streets and congregated in the city centre, waiting for the bus carrying the players and officials. Scenes like that make you realize what football can mean to people. A whole city was on parade. When we reached the square, an audience of 250,000 was waiting. The noise they made was deafening, and the Mayor struggled with difficulty through his speech. Shanks stepped forward like King Canute about to send back the waves, and as he stood in front of the microphone, the noise from the crowd increased. He called for quiet. Before the sound had died from his lips, the square was silent. It was almost supernatural, 'You,' he boomed, making a grand sweeping movement with his arm, 'you won the Cup!' The response echoed round Merseyside. The words came from his heart and were aimed at their hearts. 'Three years ago, when we came back from Wembley without the Cup, I told you we'd go back and get it for you.' There was another mighty roar of approval. 'Not only have we won the Cup on the field, we've won the Cup on the terraces, too!' We knew what we had won, but we did not know what we were about to lose.

The Master's farewell.

With Duncan McKenzie at the Arc de Triomphe.

It's there! The title breakthrough at Wolves, 1976.

13

Under new management

When first I heard that Shanks was retiring as Liverpool's manager shortly before the start of the 1974–75 season, I thought it was a joke. The shock was so great that I refused to believe it was true. I have since heard that it was not the first time Shanks had offered the club his resignation. When it happened again the chairman, John Smith, tried to talk him round to signing a new contract. The chairman did not expect a crisis, but Shanks was adamant. A board meeting was called, at which the chairman announced the news. Apparently, one of the directors, Sidney Reakes, said, 'Again? You're joking.' He stood up and was about to walk out, when the chairman replied, 'It's true, we need a new manager.' He had delayed breaking the news in the hope that Shanks could be persuaded to stay, but finally he realized that nothing would change Shanks's mind.

I have been asked to explain why he retired many times. It is a question I still ask myself. At first, in the confusion caused by the announcement, I thought back to Wembley and wondered if he was upset because the players had not taken him on their lap of honour. Perhaps he wanted to quit while he was at the top. I had a slight suspicion – and I have too high a regard for the man to even think of asking him about this – that he might have felt the team had reached its peak and would soon have been on the decline. In fact, Shanks left a team capable of replacing him, and Liverpool showed the kind of knowledge and expertise other clubs might do well to follow when they promoted Bob Paisley to manager instead of bringing in an outsider.

Bob had been a great help to Shanks over the years, and he was sensible enough not to attempt to change a sucessful system or to stamp his own personality on the team as soon as he took charge. There is still much of Shanks's character left in the Liverpool team, and Bob's triumph was the way in which he let it continue before gradually asserting himself.

I am a critic of the way a rift was allowed to develop between Shanks and the club, but there are two sides to everything. I heard rumours that Shanks had made uncomplimentary remarks about the team, but refused to believe them. I found it hard to accept that he would allow the bitterness he felt towards the board to spill over on to the players, because over the years the players had meant everything to him. Where Shanks was out of order was in not showing more tact during the early part of Bob's tenure as manager. Bob had just taken on the hardest job in football. To be replacing Bill Shankly, everybody said he was on a hiding to nothing, that he was no more than a sparring partner for a couple of rounds until the club found someone else. Some of the players thought that as well, and we wanted to help Bob in every way we could.

K.K.—H

When we went to Melwood, Shanks would be there, quite rightly using the facilities. But would not it have been better if he had used them in the afternoons, when Bob and the team were not there? The players would come into training and say, 'Good morning, Boss,' to Shanks and then greet Bob Paisley with 'Good morning, Bob.' Poor Bob must have wondered what was happening. It was an embarrassing situation. It could be argued that the facilities should have been open to Shanks, because he had built them. They were the fruits of his hard work, his ideas and his success. I just believe he should have used more discretion.

That is probably what started the aggravation. Shanks began to feel he was not wanted and the wound began to fester. Having given the managership to Bob, the club had to ensure that he was allowed to act in his own way. At the same time, they should have found a better way of dealing with Shanks. He had more than earned whatever financial security he was given, and he deserved some kind of permanent recognition. It was wrong to let a man like that just drift away, but eventually it became impossible to put the situation right. Shanks remained both loved and powerful on Merseyside, but he would have resented any offer of a recall because it had taken so long in coming. Liverpool had hurt his pride.

I will never meet another person like Shanks. I am certain he could have been a great socialist leader because he genuinely believed that people mattered above everything else. He won people over because they knew he was sincere when he said that neither he or the players was important, only the supporters and the stadium mattered. If Lord Snowdon had walked into his office, Shanks probably wouldn't have bothered too much about him, but if some lads from the Kop had walked in, he would have been as nice as pie. I think he resented the big nobs – apart from a few he really liked.

Shanks tended to be unpredictable, chatting away one day while seeming to be in a world of his own the next. That was understandable because he carried so much of the club around in his head and worked extremely hard. He arrived at Anfield at 8.30 every morning and would answer all his own mail, using a typewriter, one-finger style. At training he would watch all the time for every little change of mood among the players. If someone was injured, he would come on strong with his psychology. Liverpool is not a good club for players when they are injured. They do not encourage malingering. If a player missed training Shanks would at least hear him out, but if he thought the excuse was poor, he would say so, in no uncertain terms. If he thought the reason was valid, he would let the matter pass. If it happened again, he would remind the player that three months earlier he had used the same excuse.

You could not argue with Shanks. I remember a group of us talking about Communism, and the debate had lasted for about fifteen minutes when Shanks suddenly said, 'I would shoot the bloody lot of them!' That was the end of the discussion as far as he was concerned. An example of Shanks's changing moods was the time he sent the coach, Reuben Bennett, to watch a foreign team we were due to play. Shanks had seen them twice, and Reuben had made a report on the way they approached corner kicks and free kicks, and was due to give an overall tactical picture of the opposition. Reuben had barely started, and was stuttering over some of the strange names, when Shanks

Bob Paisley's
League title smile at
Wolverhampton.

Joy in the UEFA Cup
Final.

One against
Manchester United
at Anfield.

interrupted him and said, 'All right, Reuben, that's all we need to know – let them worry about *us!*' Before other games, we would often do a great deal of homework.

Shanks was quick to seize upon any opportunity to undermine the opposition. There was the time when a plaque – 'This is Anfield' – was placed above the tunnel leading from the dressing-rooms to the pitch. Shanks was talking to Joe Harvey, at the top of the steps leading to the tunnel, about an hour before a game against Newcastle. I was just passing by with some tickets when Malcolm Macdonald saw the plaque and said jokingly. 'I told you we had found the right place, Boss.' 'Wait till you get out there, son, and you'll know you're at Anfield,' said Shanks. 'You can run, but you canna' hide!'

The supporters responded to every wave of Shanks's hand, and it was typical of him that he should go into the Kop when Liverpool played Coventry after his retirement. When Shanks retired, he said to me, 'I want to give you this, son', and he put into my hand a small medallion in the shape of a number thirteen. He told me a woman in Prague had given it to him and said, 'Wear that, Mr Shankly, and you will never die.' I bought a strong chain for the medallion and wore it round my neck. Some time after, it came loose and went missing, during which time I went eight games without scoring a goal. I eventually found the medallion and wore it for two years, until I lost it again, this time during a match with Derby when I was not so fortunate. It was trodden into the Baseball Ground, but Derby could not find it. Again I went several matches without scoring a goal. I am not superstitious, but for a long time I felt naked without that medallion, and was most upset to have lost it. I have had some fabulous gifts in football, but that one from Shanks meant more to me than any other.

Shanks's socialist ideals were reflected in his approach to football. He demanded that the players share the work and help each other. No one player was overburdened. Although people have said Liverpool were not exciting to watch, it was true that we were built more for winning trophies than for entertaining. Normally, we played good, solid football that gradually wore other teams down and won us matches, but on our day we could entertain as much as, if not more than, any other team.

Fitness played a large part in our success, and we were trained to play strongly for the entire ninety minutes. That is why we were always so dangerous and capable of winning matches in the final ten minutes. Our reputation soon became a psychological weapon.

Liverpool have a book which the players refer to as the 'Bible'. Shanks started it and Joe Fagan now keeps it. It contains most of the secrets of Liverpool's success, showing what the team does every day of every week of every year. Our approach to training, from pre-season to the final match was logged. If we made a mistake, it was there, in black and white, for everyone to see. If we produced a winning formula, it was also there for reference. I would often hear Joe say, 'That's funny. Three years ago a similar problem cropped up, and there's the answer in the book.' The idea of a club keeping a manual might not appeal to some people, who would argue that the game is constantly changing, but the basic idea of the game – to prevent goals and save matches and to score goals and win matches – will always be the same. Shanks's book always stressed the game's simplicity.

Before the players grew accustomed to calling Bob Paisley 'Boss', their nickname for him was 'The Rat'. There was nothing personal about this, for Bob had earned the name by relating his exploits as a 'Desert Rat' during the war. When Shanks was the manager we regarded Bob as his 'hatchet' man. If something went wrong or someone was due for disciplining, Bob would be the man to intervene. Shanks would load the gun and Bob would fire the bullets. We resented him a little, because the only time we would hear from him was when something was wrong and he was on our backs. He was always lecturing us about injuries. If he caught a player kicking a ball before he had fully recovered, Bob would become very annoyed. There is nothing he does not know about injuries. He can tell if a player has cartilage trouble simply by watching him on television, and predicted that both Colin Bell and David Nish would need cartilage operations, which they did.

Technically, Bob always knew a great deal about the game, but that side of him did not come into full view until he took the manager's job. Before then he had always been shielded by Shanks. There is no question that Shanks built the club into what it is today, but he was fortunate to have good men behind him. Bob was the ideal man for Shanks to have at his right hand. Apart from his interest in horse racing, Bob is as single-minded as Shanks about football. He is totally dedicated. The most obvious difference between them was the way in which they expressed themselves. Shanks was famous for his verbal gems delivered in his sharp, distinctive Scottish accent, whereas Bob, a Geordie, did not have the same flowing style.

I will never forget Bob's first team meeting. He leant with his back against the wall of the dressing-room at Melwood, which seemed somewhat symbolic. I could not help feeling sorry for him because he looked to be in an impossible position. 'I never wanted this job in the first place,' he told us. He might have pretended he wanted to be manager, but that was not Bob's style. When the real Bob came to light we discovered that he was not the hard man we had imagined him to be. He was no soft touch, but was instead a shy, modest man who always wanted to give credit to others.

Once we got to know Bob our relationship with him was excellent and his confidence grew. To take over from Shanks and finish second in the League in his first season, as Bob did, was an impressive start, but on Merseyside that was classed as a failure. This is how big a job Bob had taken on. I was convinced by the end of his first season that things would work out well. He had taken on a job which he did not particularly want, and was doing his utmost to make a success of it. I respected him for that and the way he was going about it. Tactically, he was brilliant, but could not put it over well, and he involved the players more in the team talks. Shanks used to dominate these, but Bob encouraged the players to participate fully. Even lads who had kept quiet began to add to the discussion. Bob was big enough to accept the fact that maybe a player could give a good reason why a certain thing should be done in a certain way, and I doubt that a team of players have ever worked more closely with their manager than Liverpool did with Bob. We willed him to win the League. We wanted to win it for him, because he was trying so hard to keep up the club's high standard.

During his second season, when we won the League Championship and the UEFA Cup, we spent three days away from it all at Wrexham. We had our meals at the hotel and then were allowed to play golf or squash. Bob even let us have a drink at night.

We had never done anything like that when Shanks was the boss. Bob was willing to let the lads stamp a little of themselves on to the club's ideas. Although Shanks's Liverpool and Bob's Liverpool differed in certain ways they were basically the same – similar training, a similar style of play and similar results. Only their characters really contrasted. They were both successful in their own way.

Publicity followed Shanks. Reporters would hustle round him after a game, whether the team had played badly or won well. They would wait for the one magical quote that would bring their pieces to life. Shanks had a way of putting things, whereas Bob's statements were merely factual.

Bob has a good sense of humour, but there was one occasion, after a 1–1 draw at Leeds, when he did not appreciate our jokes. Eddie Gray had sent our defenders in all directions by dummying with his body and moving straight on with the ball. I took Joey Jones and Phil Neal to task after the game, and then Bob chipped in, 'Give me Eddie Gray in a confined space, and he wouldn't beat me.'

'I don't know about that, Boss,' came back a chorus of players.

'I'm telling you! If you put him in a confined space . . .'

We all shook our heads, but Bob's pride would not let him give in. 'I'm telling you!' We could see he was becoming annoyed. He would not have it that he could not beat Eddie Gray.

I was close to Shanks, but I became even closer to Bob. I always felt Shanks did not want people to be too close to him. If anything, the protracted business of my transfer abroad gave Bob and me a better understanding of each other. He confided in me and relieved my personal pressure. I wondered if I could have approached Shanks in the same way once I had said I wanted to go. He might have just laughed it off and not have wanted anything to do with it, but Bob knew I meant it when I approached him. He did not want me to stay against my will.

Bob helped me in many ways, and I tried to return the compliment whenever possible. If he wanted me to play in midfield, I would do it without any qualms. But we did have one row. On the morning of the day we left for Bruges for the second leg of the UEFA Cup Final – to clinch our second League and UEFA Cup double – I was talking with Ken Addison, who runs the club's development organizations. I had heard that Ken was not travelling with us and asked why he had not been invited. 'Well, I have really,' said Ken, 'but they didn't invite my wife, so I'm not going. It's as simple as that.' That annoyed me, because Ken did a wonderful job for the players. He was only too willing to help by supplying souvenirs for children in hospital and that sort of thing. I knew some other wives had been invited, and that there were some spare tickets which were being offered to a variety of people. I went to the boss and said, 'I hope you don't mind me saying this, but I'm a bit sick about Ken Addison.'

'Why? What's up?'

'Well, he does a lot of work for the lads and takes a lot of pressure off them, and I would have thought he would have been a certainty to have been invited along with his wife.'

'Ken Addison doesn't like flying,' replied Bob.

This was true, but it did not alter the fact that Ken's wife had not been invited.

He had not even had the opportunity to decline an invitation. I spoke forcefully to Bob. 'I think it's a disgrace,' I said. 'Extra pressmen and all sorts are being asked to make up the numbers, and there is a fellow who is very much a part of this club and has this club at heart who is not being invited. I think it's disgusting. Just typical of this club. It's little things like that they fall down on.'

Bob reacted by saying that, 'It's none of your business.'

'Right,' I thundered, 'there are a lot of other things round here that are not going to be my business any more,' and I stormed out.

Some people will agree that it was not my business, but I cared about fellows like Ken Addison, and it angered me when I felt they were being left out of something. If it was right for Bob to ask my opinion about team affairs, as he did from time to time, why was it wrong for me to be concerned about someone else who mattered to the players? I did not speak to Bob on the flight and never said a word during the team talk. It was hard, because I liked the man, he was attempting to win the second leg of a double, and I thought, 'If we lose he'll think I wasn't trying for him.' As it happened, that made me play all the harder, and we did win, but I could not bring myself to make a fuss of him. I just said, 'Well done, you deserve it,' and that was that.

ABOVE With Bobby Moore in America.

Peter Taylor laughs as I take a ducking from Gordon Hill.

BELOW Look, no hands!

With Mickey Channon, Gerry Francis and the chairman of Watford.

Taxi! Mickey Channon in the driving seat, with Mike Doyle and Phil Neal on the bonnet.

14

The Belgrade boot boys

I defy anybody who has met Joe Mercer to say a nasty word about him. You have to love the man. Like most managers, he could be faulted here and there, but I shall always remember his patience and the way he helped me out of a dangerous situation.

Joe brought me back into the England team during his term in 1974 as caretaker manager between the sacking of Sir Alf Ramsey and the appointment of Don Revie. We drew 2–2 at Wembley with Argentina, who were on their way to the World Cup in Germany, and beat Wales 2–0 in Cardiff and Northern Ireland 1–0 at Wembley. Joe left me out of the team at Hampden Park, where the Scots, having qualified for the World Cup Finals, added to their confidence by beating England 2–0. He was not a tough disciplinarian. People respected Joe rather than feared him, and the good-humoured, relaxed atmosphere he brought to the England camp was reflected in the way we played during the summer tour of East Germany, Bulgaria and Yugoslavia.

We drew 1–1 in Leipzig and won 1–0 in Sofia, fine results by any standards, especially at a time when the nation was mourning our failure to qualify for the World Cup. We were then ready for the last leg before returning home. With three days to go before this final game, Joe allowed us to have a few lagers and stay up late playing cards. Next day, as soon as the plane taking us from Sofia to Belgrade had left the runway, I felt tired. 'Miss me out of the card school, I'm going for a sleep,' I said, and moved towards the rear of the plane to settle myself across some vacant seats among the pressmen. I borrowed a coat from one of them and slept soundly all the way.

When we arrived, wearing casuals instead of uniforms and feeling in a jovial mood, we laughed and joked while waiting to go through passport control. The usual procedure was for the players and officials to go first, followed by the pressmen, but on this occasion, journalist Bob Harris of Thomson Regional Newspapers, went ahead of everyone else. Frank Worthington, or 'Roy Rogers' as we called him because he walked like a cowboy, ambled through control, but was halted abruptly by a thick plate of glass which he had mistaken for an opening. We made the most of this, pressing our noses up against the glass and pulling faces at Frank.

Alec Lindsay and I then passed through control and wandered a few yards over to a conveyor belt. I was carrying two bags of beautiful pottery I had bought in Bulgaria for only about £1.50 a set. One was intended for Mum and the other for Jean. I sat down on the wooden edge of the conveyor belt, and Alec began to fool around. He climbed on to the belt and started walking the wrong way, like a character in a silent movie. He looked funny and I was laughing at him, when one of the guards came over, took hold of Alec and threw him against a brick wall. Alec staggered, fell, picked himself up and walked away. I was doubled up laughing. I couldn't help myself because it had looked like a scene straight out of a comedy script. Hardly had I collected myself when I was suddenly grabbed from behind, squeezed and lifted off the ground. The carrier bags split and the crockery spilled out, smashing on the floor. My instinctive reaction was to shrug off whoever was holding me. At first, I wondered if it was one of the players messing around, but the brute force of the attack soon made me realize something more sinister was happening. As I struggled, in a state of shock, an armed guard appeared in front of me and joined the attack. I can recall the blur of arms and the pain as I was punched and gripped around the neck. Bob Harris saw the whole thing and immediately ran to find Joe Mercer and the Football Association officials. I could feel myself being dragged away, choking from the power of the guard's arms around my neck. Mickey Channon ran across and asked what he could do. 'If I were you I'd get out of the way,' I spluttered.

I was hauled roughly into a back office and forced to kneel like a prisoner of war. Then the battering began. One guard took particular delight in administering it. I was punched, clubbed and kicked, and when I thought he had stopped, he came across and repeated the treatment again. My green trousers were covered in blood. There was no communication, just a series of grunts to accompany the blows. I am not easily scared, but I was shivering and shaking in that room.

While I was being beaten up a list of trumped-up charges were prepared. I seemed to be kneeling for a lifetime, but it finally amounted to only twenty minutes. The accusations against me were sexually assaulting an air-hostess on the flight from Sofia, assaulting a security guard, disturbing the peace and causing an obstruction. Thanks to Bob Harris, the FA officials had been able to take immediate steps to rescue me and when word reached my office prison that I was an England footballer, the attitude of the guards changed dramatically. The very men who had attacked me so eagerly, began to wipe the blood off my face, but they had done such a good job with their fists and boots that it was impossible to make me look anything other than a mess. Joe Mercer, Ted Croker, the FA Secretary, and Sir Andrew Stephen the FA Chairman, were eventually allowed into the room and shown the list of 'crimes'. Someone from the Yugoslav FA explained what I was supposed to have done. From what I could gather in my dazed condition, the guards were insisting I had struck one of them. Ted Croker and Sir Andrew Stephen demanded my immediate release, but that was not the way to approach those Yugoslavs, who were not going to bend easily.

The players wanted to pull out of the match and return home, but Joe told them, 'They've told us that if you go home, Kevin stays.' He handled the situation well. It took the FA an hour of serious talking before the guards reluctantly agreed to my release, but my fears remained even when I left that dreadful room. At the hotel I kept expecting a heavy hand to fall on my shoulder and a voice to say 'Keegan, you're under arrest!' I had been to Belgrade before with Liverpool, staying at the same hotel, and now became conscious of what had happened in the past to unsuspecting British tourists, who had often been imprisoned for nothing more than plane-spotting. I began to understand how hopeless the situation must have been for them.

Joe knew how upset I was, and asked, 'Do you want to play against them?' 'Yes,' I said, determined not to be bullied into submission. The incident at the airport was glossed over by the local papers, and there was no reaction from the crowd when I walked out for the match. We drew 2–2 and I managed to score the equalizer in the last few minutes. I was delighted to do that for Joe, because it gave the team an unbeaten tour record. Yugoslavia were also one of the fancied teams for the World Cup.

When we arrived back at the airport I caught site of the brute who had given me such a beating. I swear that if I had had a gun I would have shot him. I will never forget his face.

I feared that I would not be allowed to leave, right up until the plane took off. I resolved never to return. During the return journey we talked more freely about the affair. The big joke concerned the air-hostess. 'If I'm going to get arrested for something like that, then at least I want the pleasure of having done it,' I told the lads. Then I thought again, 'Imagine anyone really wanting to rape one of them—half of them look like men, anyway!'

Whenever Alec and I were on a trip abroad together after that, I would tell him to 'keep away from me!' I would like to forget about the whole incident, but it is not possible. Up until now I have always tried to gloss over it, because it is not something I really want to talk about. When I arrived home I was surprised at the number of people who said, 'I see you've been in trouble again,' as if it was my fault. As far as trouble was concerned, the season was only beginning.

Celebrating the League Championship triumph
with Dad at Wolverhampton.

Dynamic duo?

Carlisle's Peter Carr gets there first.

With the Charity Shield, UEFA Cup and League Championship trophy.

On the Kop.

15

Rough justice

Liverpool played a tour match at Kaiserslautern, West Germany, as part of their preparation for the start of the 1974–75 season, and one of the Germans made a dangerous tackle on Ray Kennedy. The incident infuriated us, and half our team charged towards the culprit. The referee moved in, singled me out, and I was sent off. I could not believe it, I had done nothing. Fortunately, Liverpool supported me when I pleaded my innocence, and no further action was taken against me by the Football Association. This little affair in Kaiserslautern was nothing compared with what followed.

Within a week of the match in West Germany, we were back at Wembley for the Charity Shield game, Liverpool against Leeds United. I think people underestimated how much pressure was on the teams that day. As soon as Leeds and Liverpool were put on the same pitch one could forget about charity. Leeds had pipped us for the League Championship. They had gone more than half the season without losing a game, and only one team had chased them – Liverpool. At one stage, we were within two points of catching them, then we lost a game and the gap opened again. Leeds won with sixty-two points and we were runners-up with fifty-seven. We had regained a great deal of ground after making a bad start to the season and won the FA Cup. The year before we had won the League Championship and the UEFA Cup. While we had won three trophies in three years, Leeds had won two – the FA Cup in 1972 and the Championship in 1974 – and had been close in several others.

Shanks had retired, and was to lead out Liverpool at Wembley for the last time. Don Revie had taken the England job, and took a seat in the stand to watch Brian Clough take his place at the head of his former team. This was to be *the* confrontation. It was like two of the world's greatest boxers, arch rivals, being asked to give an exhibition bout. I recall Bob Paisley saying, 'I'm a bit worried about this. It's a bad time to have a game like this. It's far too early. Just go out there and knock the ball about and try to enjoy yourselves.' Bob was right. It was a bad time to have so much pressure. There was only a week to go to the start of the season and the players were not mentally attuned for a game which was supposed to decide which team was the best in England. Those people who believed the players would ease off for a charity show did not know Bill Shankly and Don Revie, who both remained very much the influence behind their former players. They also did not cater for Billy Bremner and Kevin Keegan, Ian Callaghan and Johnny Giles, and Norman Hunter and Emlyn Hughes.

We set out to do what Bob had asked. We wanted to win and put on a good show for the fans, but the game had barely started when there was a nasty incident which brought some ill feeling into the game. The player responsible was Allan Clarke. I do not hate many players, and though I don't dislike Clarkie as a person, I cannot stand him as a footballer. He is a fine player, and I envy his finishing in front of goal, but other aspects of his play infuriate me. His tackling for instance. When Phil Thompson went to clear the ball upfield from the Liverpool defence, there was a touch of the old Clarkie I knew so well. The referee obviously didn't see what Clarkie did and, to toss a thought into the old debate over whether or not ex-players would make better referees than non-players, I will emphasize that the referee that day was an ex-player, Bob Matthewson.

In spite of Clarkie's tackle, we settled down to play some good football, knocking the ball smartly around the field and in behind Gordon McQueen and Norman Hunter. Bremner and Giles could not seem to match the pace of our game. We were half-a-yard faster, and Leeds were lucky to be no more than one goal down at half-time.

'Just keep it up, lads,' was all Bob had to say to us during the interval. I do not know what was said in the Leeds dressing-room, but as soon as the second half started, even the players who were not noted for kicking were having a go at us. All the top teams can be hard in a subtle fashion, and Leeds were past masters of the art. I am not suggesting that they were openly brutal, but they were accomplished in the technical, or 'professional', foul. Liverpool were more physical when Tommy Smith and Larry Lloyd were together in the defence. They could both look after themselves, and also take care of team-mates who perhaps were not so capable. They were hard, though, as I have stressed before, Smith took more hard knocks than he gave.

Players have to be adaptable. If a man is marking someone and playing him dead right but is still unable to get a foot in at the ball or shake his opponent with some occasional bodily contact, then, if he is a good professional, he will readjust his game. Otherwise he will be totally ineffective. I'm not complaining about this, because it is all part of the game. It may surprise some people that I actually enjoyed playing against Norman Hunter. I voted for him when he won the Professional Footballers' Association Player of the Year award, and, for me, he could have won that award every year. Norman could kick when he felt it was necessary – that was part of his makeup – but he did not get enough credit for his skill. He could flight the ball so accurately with his left foot. Norman was respected in the profession because he used his assets to the full. He could be both skilful and hard. He lived by the sword, but he was also prepared to die by it, which was another aspect of the man I liked. He has kicked me and I have kicked him. I have hurt myself doing it, but I have probably hurt him, too, and we would not complain about it. I travelled a hundred miles from my home in Wales to play in his testimonial match, and the first thing he did was to chop me down. Norman was not prepared to change, no matter what happened. There were times when he made tackles I did not approve of, but at the end of the day or the end of the season, I had to hold up my hand and say he was a great player.

Leeds could foul beautifully, but surely the onus was on referees to protect the innocent. Too often in matches – and Leeds were by no means the only offenders – a bad tackle early on would bring no more than a finger-wagging from a referee. Players could be put out of the game before they had even got into their stride, and yet referees would wait until a hour or so had elapsed and then suddenly panic because the game was getting out of hand. They might then book or send-off some poor player who had done no real harm. It seemed as though teams were invited to have one free kick at any player on the opposing side early in the game.

At Wembley, Leeds became aggressive. Giles was on the ball and I went after him. He tried to turn, and, though I was close to him, he shielded the ball so well that I could not get in a good tackle, and he bumped into me. The referee awarded a foul, and Giles thumped me. 'Come here,' said Bob Matthewson, but I said, 'Don't send him off, it was only on the spur of the moment.' I pleaded for Giles, who was booked. Shortly after that, Bremner took a dig at me as he ran past, and then he slipped. If he had not slipped I would not have gone after him, but I had been provoked twice and was so annoyed about it that I thought I would repay him. I got hold of Billy, aimed a blow at him, and he aimed one back. I was sent-off though I still maintain that I was provoked. I was even more upset at the manner in which Bob Matthewson dealt with the incident. If he had simply said, 'Off you go,' I could have accepted it better, but he towered above Billy and me and he treated us like a couple of school-children. 'It's a good game,' he said. 'It's going well, and you two are spoiling it – so go and get a bath.'

There I was, being ordered off a pitch for the second time in a week. I was blameless in West Germany, and at Wembley I had simply shown Leeds that I had had enough of their niggling. I admit that my action had been wrong, but I had not hurt anyone. It was not as if I had tried to break someone's leg. 'Come off it, Bob, you're joking,' I said. 'Off,' he insisted. When I reached the dressing-room I realized I had taken off my shirt. I cannot think why I did that. Strange things can happen to people who are under pressure.

What I did was stupid, but having admitted that, could there have been a logical reason for it? I felt I had been made a fool of by the referee. I did not like that, but I accepted it and I went off. I did not refuse to leave, which would have been worse. Looking back, I suppose I could argue that knowing the game had finished for me, it was quite natural to take off my shirt. But in the middle of Wembley? There was not any reason for it. I did not know Billy Bremner had also taken off his shirt. I would have thought he had less reason to do so than I had. It could only have been because I had done it, which was really no reason at all. We were childish.

As I left the field, five people rose from their seats in the stand – my Mum and Dad, my brother Mike, Jean and Dad's mate, Harry Wadsley. The game was also finished for them. Dad came into the dressing-room. I was still in my shorts. 'Don't worry about it,' he said. 'Well, it's over now,' I said. 'It was just one of those things.' Though I have since replayed the incident over and over again in my mind, I did not give it a lot of thought at the time. Bremner came into the room just as I was about to dress. The affair had obviously affected him more than me, because he was almost in tears. 'Sorry,' he said. 'It's all right,' I told him.

'Bugger off!' said Dad.

'It's no good being annoyed with the fellow, Dad,' I said. 'He's as sick as I am.' I suppose it was natural for people to assume that Billy and I would be at each other's

Incident at Wembley. Bob Matthewson lays down the law and Gordon McQueen joins the Keegan–Bremner chorus of protest.

Topless and heading for trouble.

No charity at Wembley ... but a restraining arm from Norman Hunter.

throats after what had happened, but I did not feel any animosity towards him and I know he did not feel any towards me. Before I left Wembley I went to see Shanks. He had only one more game left for Liverpool, which was to be Billy McNeill's testimonial at Celtic the following Monday. 'I'm sorry about what happened, Boss,' I said. 'I'm going home. I want to think about things.' 'All right, son,' he replied.

The Liverpool players went to Glasgow and I went to a night-club in Doncaster and drowned my sorrows with the owner, Mick Wise, a friend of mine. I am not a heavy drinker, and do not get drunk, but I downed a few that night. Shanks must have had second thoughts, because at about one o'clock in the morning I saw a face I recognized. Maurice Setters, then manager of Doncaster Rovers, came into the club and was obviously pleased to see me. He told he had been looking for me for about three hours and must have been in every pub in Doncaster. 'Shanks phoned me,' he said. 'You'd better give him a ring. He wants you to play in Glasgow and he's going to wait up until you phone.' I phoned Shanks from the club and he did ask me to play. I had too much respect for him to refuse, and, in any case, I was beginning to forget about what had happened. I soon get over things. You have to keep bouncing back when anything gets the better of you. I am constantly being reminded that football is a great life, but I sometimes wonder how many people would be able to cope with the abuse and the insults which accompany the glory.

When I arrived at Parkhead, Jock Stein took me to one side and said, 'I'm glad you came, because these people up here want to see you play and it's in times of trouble that your true character shows itself.' It was the best test I could have had. Shanks wanted so badly for us to win, and at least we managed to draw for him. Both teams played as if they were trying to prove something, but in the right spirit. We had by far the better of the first half and then they began to get on top in the second half. I had been somewhat sceptical about going to Glasgow, but I am glad I did, for Shanks and for Jock Stein.

Back at Liverpool, I continued training and waited for the heavy hand of football discipline: MAKE EXAMPLES OF THEM!

I made a point not to read the papers, because I knew Billy and I were in for it, but it was difficult to escape from the publicity surrounding our case. Being sent off with Billy Bremner did not help me. We had to be given the same sentence, I am not denying that, but it was something new for me, whereas Billy had been sent off several times. He had been through it before, and I felt we would be judged on his record rather than mine. If we had been two young lads who had never been sent off before ... if we had been sent off at Hartlepool and not at Wembley.

If...

What chance had we against the increasing pressure of public opinion? A boy had been stabbed near a tea bar during half-time at a match at Blackpool, football hooliganism was rife, and referees had been told to clamp down on players. Justice had to be seen to be done and we were the scapegoats.

Bob Paisley came with me to the hearing. Shanks has said that if he had been there he would have got me off, but I am sceptical. Billy was represented by Maurice Lindley, the Leeds assistant manager. We might as well have stayed at home, because I am convinced that the sentences were all but typed up before we even entered the room. It was a farce from start to finish. We were shown a letter which had been passed on to the Football Association by the Home Office. In the letter, an MP strongly advised that we should be banned for life. 'What's this got to do with us?' asked Bob. 'We're here about football. That's politics.' It was a clear indication of the political pressure brought to bear on our case.

Vernon Stokes, the chairman of the Commission, told me I had done wrong. This was the same Vernon Stokes that had been suspended *sine die* for irregularities when he was chairman of Portsmouth. Sir Matt Busby, another of the Commission, said our behaviour might encourage soccer hooliganism. I wanted to say, 'Put your own house in order before you talk to me about soccer hooliganism,' but I was able to choke back the words. Busby is a great man, and when I met him socially I found that he more than matched up to his image. At that time, however, I felt bitter towards everybody, especially those sitting in judgement. I was terrified in case I said something that would land me even deeper in trouble. If I had said what I wanted to say I might have been banned *sine die*! I just told them I was sorry for what I had done.

There was an interval while the 'judge and jury' deliberated in private. As we waited, Billy said to me, 'What do you think?'

I said, 'We're going to be made examples of – we're going to pay for many people's sins, not just ours. I reckon we can forget about football for a good few matches.'

We were suspended for eleven matches and fined £500 each. Some of the people who had almost begged for us to be thrown to the lions then said how harsh the FA were!

When we returned to Liverpool, Bob Paisley asked, 'What do you want to do?' 'I just want to get as far away from here as I can,' I said. 'The last thing I want to do is train with the lads all week and then have no game on the Saturday.' With five weeks to make use of, I decided initially to take a golfing holiday in Bournemouth, which did me the world of good, walking over the fairways, far away from crowds and publicity. I then went home to Doncaster and urged my father to visit a specialist. He had been ill for some time, but was reluctant to go to hospital and leave Mum on her own. 'I'm home now, so I can look after Mum,' I said.

Dad had a check-up, and was told that he had a tumour and needed an operation if he was to live for more than six months. When I made inquiries at a local hospital, I was asked if we wanted the operation under the National Health Service or to have my father taken in as a private patient. I asked what difference that would make, and was told that he might have to wait up to eighteen months under the Health Service. We could have left it for a few months and Dad might have been given a bed, but he might have died during that time. I paid for my father to have private treatment. I am not praising myself. I could never again spend money to greater effect. Any son would have taken the same course. It was the best thing I ever did. But if I had not been in a position to raise the money, what would Dad have done then? I was annoyed with the system. Dad was typical of many people. All his life, he had done everything by the book, and yet he would not have been guaranteed a hospital bed immediately he needed it unless I had paid.

Dad made a deal with me. 'I'll go to hospital if you marry that lass of yours, he said. 'You've kept her waiting long enough.' That surprised me, because Jean and I had talked about getting married at the end of the season, and I thought my parents would have objected because Jean was still so young. Perhaps they were worried because I had been sent off twice in a week and thought I might be getting into bad habits! Jean and I telephoned her parents from a coin box in Liverpool and told them we wanted to get married as soon as possible. The last thing we wanted was a big fuss, so we kept our plans secret and were married within a fortnight. My sister Mary booked the reception in her married name, Mary Cooke, at our favourite little restaurant in Doncaster. It was big enough to accommodate fourteen guests – my Mum and Dad; Jean's Mum and Dad; my brother Mike; my sister Mary; her husband, Russ, and two children, Sharon and Lynne; Jean's brother, Colin, with his wife, Ann, and their little girl, Helen; the photographer, Harry Ormesher; and the priest.

Jean had the most difficult job. When she went to choose her wedding dress at a shop in Liverpool she used an assumed name – Lillian Roberts, after her landlady – for 'security' reasons. We told a great many white lies in order to keep our secret. Jean told the girls at the tax office that she was going to college, but felt so ashamed of herself that she confided in her best friend: 'I'm getting married tomorrow, would you wait until eleven o'clock in the morning and say to the other girls "Jean's just getting married" and apologize to them for me?' They were very understanding about it. Word somehow reached the reporters, but when they went to see Mum she said, 'No, you must be joking! Are you getting mixed up with George Best?'

People even telephoned Jean's Mum and Dad in Newquay. 'We hear your daughter is getting married.'

'Is she?' said Dad. 'I'm sure I'd know if she was getting married ...'

We told so many white lies that we had to pray for forgiveness.

Jean told me about a conversation she had some time earlier with Emlyn Hughes's wife, Barbara, who told her that they had tried to keep their wedding secret, but they still had coach loads of people from Liverpool turning up at the church. I was determined that it was going to be Jean's day as well as mine and not a day for well-meaning fans.

We were married at St Peter in Chains Roman Catholic Church, Doncaster, on 23 September 1974. Jean wore a beautiful white dress with an enormous train, and had one bridesmaid, Gill Roberts. There were swing doors at the entrance to the church, and when Jean arrived her father held one door and Gill the other. Jean's train was so long that she was almost at the altar before her father caught up with her again! I wore a white leather suit which Jean, at first glance, thought was linen. When the priest asked us to sit, we did so on stools covered by leather. The seat of my trousers stuck to the top of the stool, and there was a most embarrassing sound when I rose again. Jean and I looked at each other and laughed. Unfortunately, we had no time for a honeymoon. The next day I was training at Melwood and Jean was back to work.

Jean and I love children and plan to have a family, but life became so hectic that we decided to wait a while. When the players' wives went to Bruges for the UEFA Cup Final, they spent an evening talking about their children, as wives do. Jean listened

Bride and groom.

with interest and eventually one of the girls thought to ask, 'And how are your dogs, Jean?' That became a standing joke. We share everything, including problems, and she takes half the strain away from me. At times we are more like best friends than man and wife. We have arguments, of course, but we have never slept in separate rooms, and we do not sulk at each other.

Dad had his operation and Jean and I got married, so at least some good came of that bad day at Wembley, although I kidded Jean by saying, 'It was bad enough getting suspended for five weeks and being fined £500, but getting married as well – that was a triple blow!'

Any old iron?

Tally ho!

A sprint with Hadleigh.

A house of our own.

We love Paris.

16

At odds with the Revs

I don't care what others say, I still believe Don Revie is the right man for the England job. I don't think there is anyone around at the moment who is better qualified to do it.

No one has been more depressed than I have by some of our results and performances. Instead of being a welcome change from club matches and lifting my spirits, the games against the Republic of Ireland, Finland, Italy and Holland knocked me down. But I blamed the players, not Revie.

We have let down the supporters and we have also let down our manager. It's all very well for people to talk about systems and so on, but the players Revie has picked have been lads of proven ability who have just not been able to deliver for him. Once a man has prepared his squad and picked his team, he can only say to the players, 'You know what you do at club level, so do it for me at this level. That's all I want. I only want your club form.' Those have been the Revs' words, but the players have not always responded to them. The only player who knocked the Revs publicly was Alan Ball, and I reckon Ballie did a Judas on England in a newspaper article shortly before our game in Rome. He said he hoped England lost against Italy. That, coming from a fellow who had captained the side a year earlier, did more harm to our morale than any amount of criticism by journalists.

Ballie was also quoted by a newspaper as saying that I shouldn't captain the side, which is open to argument. Of the group of players we had together at the time, I felt I was the right man for the job, but my feeling is that at international level the captain is someone who calls the toss of a coin. I captained England against Finland when we were terrible, against Italy when we were terrible and against Holland when we were terrible. I couldn't turn round and rollick players for not working hard, because they did, and if a lad's having a bad day, he knows it better than I do. Plus the fact that we were so bad that I didn't know where to start to put it right. Having made these points about Ballie, I must stress that I have tremendous admiration for him as a player, and when he captained England he was a good leader.

I will agree that it was a pity the Revs couldn't have stuck to the side we had in America for the Bicentennial tournament during the summer of 1976 – Clemence, Todd, Doyle, Thompson, Mills, Gerry Francis, Cherry, Brooking, myself, Pearson and Channon, augmented by Greenhoff, Taylor, Rimmer, Corrigan, Clement, Neal, Towers, Wilkins, Royle and Hill. Eight of those players knew they were virtually sure of being in the team, and it showed in their confidence when they went out on to the

Navigating for the Revs.

With Peter Cormack.

ENG–LAND!

field. But in no time the team was completely unsettled, so much so that I used to think, 'God knows what the next one's going to be.' I could be captain for one match and not be sure of my place in the next, which was a diabolical situation for an international player to be in. Injuries didn't help, and when players with ability failed to produce form, the Revs had no alternative but to leave them out.

The press played their part. I know it is wrong for a person to allow himself to be forced into things, but I believe the press forced the Revs to pick certain players. For instance, they had the flags out for Charlie George – 'Charlie's the boy!' . . . 'By George – he's back!' – then after Charlie had been selected and failed to live up to their expectations, the press boys dropped him quicker than they had picked him up.

I think the Revs should have left open a few floating places in the side while establishing a nucleus of players. But it is always easy to talk after the event. For example, when we played Holland it was obvious for weeks that Trevor Francis had to play because he deserved a chance. Stan Bowles had played in only one game and it would have been unfair to have judged him on the performance in Italy, so either Mickey Channon or myself had to go out. If the Revs had left me out he couldn't have hurt me more than he did by leaving out Mickey, because we are such good friends, but that's football. We all knew Mickey would be back.

Before the game, it was the right team, but after the game it was the wrong team, because we didn't win. Holland scored an early goal and then they scored another, and suddenly it was exhibition stuff for them. I know what it's like, because Liverpool would crucify the opposition given a 2–0 lead like that, and that's exactly what Holland did to England. Everything became desperate for England, and all the pressure was lifted off the Dutch. They could knock the ball about and create even more chances.

Cruyff took the match over and his performance contrasted sharply to the games he played for Barcelona against Liverpool, especially the one at Anfield when he acted more like a manager than a member of the team and even supervised the substitutions. On that occasion he did more talking and gesturing than playing, and I wondered if he'd reached the stage where he had so much security off the field that his game had begun to suffer. I'm not saying his substitutions were not good ones, but it struck me that he was taking some dignity away from men he had to play alongside. That is my only criticism of Cruyff. How can you criticize a player who is so brilliant on the field?

While Cruyff seemed to have the freedom of Wembley, I struggled along with the other England players, though most people tended to overlook the fact that the Dutch had assigned Neeskens, one of the best players in the world, to forsake his normal midfield job and mark me out of the match.

The Revs is resented because of what he did at Leeds, mainly because he was so successful. When a person is successful in our line of business he tends to be disliked, because people grow tired of the same faces dominating the game and ache for someone new to arrive. It happened to Leeds and it happened to Liverpool. People gave us credit for our achievements and respected us for them, but inside they were dying for someone else to win the League.

The way the Revs achieved his success was not always seen to be the right way, but nevertheless the man did a job and did it to the utmost of his ability. He was accused of kicking his way out of the Second Division, but he obviously assessed what Leeds needed to win promotion.

Maybe they were a bit physical, but their play took them where they wanted to go. We English are not particularly good at giving credit to our own people. We love to praise Helmut Schoen and Miljan Miljanic and knock Alf Ramsey and Don Revie.

To be honest, I hated Leeds and everything they stood for. Being a Liverpool player, I had to hate Leeds, because they were our biggest rivals. I almost hated the Revs because, as the manager of Leeds, he was my natural enemy. When he took over England I was worried. I had the feeling that I wouldn't be his kind of player and I thought my international career was finished. I was wrong.

Joe Mercer gave me a fresh start, but it was the Revs who provided the missing link in my career and really made me into an international player. That was after a shaky start to our relationship, when I walked out on him.

The build-up to that incident started when England were due to play Northern Ireland in Belfast. I had scored the goal in our previous match, when we had won 1–0 in Cyprus in a far from impressive performance, which left few of the players confident of retaining their places.

'We want to go to Belfast,' said the Revs, when the squad gathered for the Home Championship matches. 'But if any of you lads don't fancy going because of the situation over there just say so now and we'll understand.'

We all wanted to go, because we knew the Irish people were keen to see us play and we firmly believed that we would be safe, but on the Thursday the Revs took me to one side at our London headquarters, and said, 'How would you like a weekend at home?'

'Are you trying to tell me I'm dropped?' I asked.

'No, no, I wouldn't do that, you were one of the few successes,' he said. 'But it's only fair to tell you that the FA have had a letter which says that if you go to Ireland you'll be shot. Quite honestly, we want you to play, but we can't make that decision for you. We'll not take the risk. I'll tell the press you're injured, but you'll be straight back into the team for the other games because you're an important part of my plans.'

I was sick about being left out and not a bit worried about the threat. I've always been inclined to be even more determined to do something when I've been warned off, and I wanted to play in Belfast more than ever. For one reason, Liverpool have so many fans there. I was wary in a professional sense, because if you give up your place in a team the chap who replaces you might play well enough to put you back to square one. I wasn't prepared to risk that for the sake of what I felt was the work of a crank.

After talking with the Revs, I telephoned Jean and told her about the threat.

'What are you going to do?' she said.

'Well, the boss has told me I can come home if I want to, but I really want to play. It took me a long time to get a regular place.'

'Well, look,' said Jean. 'I know what I think, but I know the way you think and it won't do me any good telling you what I think.'

I'm stubborn. I went back to the Revs and said, 'I've talked it over with my wife and she said it's up to me, and I want to play. I don't want to give up my position.'

'Great,' he said. 'That's what I wanted you to say, but I couldn't say it for you.'

The game was a goalless draw, a disappointing result and performance for us, and we returned from Belfast to prepare for the next match, against Wales at Wembley.

After training on the Tuesday, the Revs read out the team. I waited for my name to be called out, but it wasn't. I was upset, because I had run all over the field for him in Cyprus and I had shown how keen I was to keep my place by going to Belfast when my life had been threatened. But I accepted the fact that he had to experiment and waited for him to talk things over with me.

The team had been announced at about 11.30 am and I waited and waited, but nothing happened. I became obsessed by the thought that the Revs was using me as a mug, playing me in away games, where everyone has to run and work and tighten up – in other words, do the sort of things natural forwards don't enjoy very much – and dropping me in favour of the ball player when the bonus of a game at Wembley came along. I don't mean that as an insult to Dave Thomas, who took my place against Wales, but I had the impression that I was being strung along, and I didn't like it.

At six o'clock I packed my bags. I joined in the squad's bingo session, but when the putting competition started I decided I had waited long enough. The Revs had seen me around the hotel often enough since the morning, so I collected my bags and left. I still believe I was right on principle to react to the snub and to fear that I would become the away match work horse to be sacrificed for home games, but I'm sorry I walked out. I realize I should have gone to the Revs and told him how I felt.

He telephoned and asked me to rejoin the squad. That was big of him, because if I'd been in his position, I wouldn't have telephoned and I wouldn't have been so forgiving.

'What happened is forgotten,' he promised, and he kept his word. Before the next game, against Scotland, I saw that I was sharing a room with Kevin Beattie, another player who had once walked out on England. 'I see, you think Kev and I are going to plan it properly and walk out together this time, do you?' I joked, and fortunately the affair ended with a laugh. Everyone makes mistakes and everyone has upsets and the better men are the ones who can forget them and not hold grudges.

Much has been made of the Revs' painstaking study of opponents. There was the joke that when he travelled with Manchester United to Italy for their game against Juventus his filing cabinet wouldn't fit on the plane. But I could imagine the criticism if he didn't do his homework. He is very thorough, very professional, and there is not a thing we do not know about the opposition. England play, on average, about eight games a year and it is the manager's business to know what we will be up against.

He prepares dossiers, the players read them, we go through them as a team, and that's all there is to it. The Revs is very good at technical talks. He is like Shanks. He builds it up, and he doesn't need the dossiers for those. But imagine if we didn't have the dossiers and we slipped up because of a couple of free kicks, where would that leave him?

Not being superstitious myself, I can't see how trivial rituals can help a football team. It doesn't matter which suit you wear, how you tie your laces, which boot you fasten first, which shirt you wear, or what position in line you take when the team runs out on to the field, because all that matters is your performance against the opposition. I wouldn't like to be caught up in superstitions because one thing leads to another and suddenly you find yourself lost in a world of superstition and forget what the game is all about. I'm not saying that applies to the Revs. He has grown up with his superstitions, and if you are that way inclined, fair enough. His superstitions have never bothered me.

He works with the team immediately before a match. He shares the emotions and lets us know he will be out there playing with us in spirit. He doesn't just stand around in his suit spouting a load of tactics, he takes off his jacket and his shirt and helps with the massage. He helps to tone the players and offers words of encouragement. He is always the first to give praise.

Fun has been made of his bingo sessions and putting competitions, like the joke about the fellow called up for the first time to an England squad who was told by an experienced player, 'You don't have to play particularly well or score many goals, but if you are putting well and can win a few houses of bingo you've got a great chance!' But I think the bingo and the putting brought the players together more than anything else the Revs did, especially the putting. It's surprising how the spirit develops when lads are competing for prizes. We even run a book on it, with the boss and I sharing the role of bookmaker.

Once we lost £455 to Mickey Channon and Trevor Brooking. Ballie used to keep the book with the boss, but when Ballie was left out of the squad I took the job. During the tour of America I began assessing the odds. Mike Doyle was a good putter, so he was 6–1. Brian Greenhoff was also good enough to be rated 6–1 along with coach Bill Taylor, with 5–1 against Les Cocker, the Revs' assistant, 7 or 8–1 against me and 8–1 against the boss. After that the odds tended to widen.

By the time we reached Helsinki, where we beat Finland 4–1, Mickey Channon was a 75–1 chance. He's rubbish at putting. He doesn't even know how to hold a putter. He doesn't play golf, in fact he's really interested only in horses. If he was allowed to putt while sitting on a horse, he'd probably do better. Mickey backed himself with £5 and Trevor put £2 on Mickey. We took in £70, but we'd won £30 in Los Angeles and £45 in New York and £40 in Philadelphia, so we felt we could afford to splash the odds a bit. But Mickey reached the final and I was nervous, because he was playing Norman Medhurst, of Chelsea, the physiotherapist, so he had a chance. Norman's putting was not much better.

We would make up titles for people, like Scruffiest Dresser of the Week and Worst Five-a-Side player, and Norman wore a T-shirt with 'I Love The Boss' printed on it, so he was voted Crawler of the Week. We kept saying to him, 'Are you going to sit next to the boss, Norman?' He had putted well to reach the final, but then his touch deserted him with the pressure on, and Mickey won 7–0.

'Right, Norman,' I said. 'I've lost more than £200 and I hope you've enjoyed yourself, because the way the boss is looking at you, this could be your last trip!'

I turned to the Revs and said, jokingly, 'And if you want me for the next match you'll have to double the international fee!'

That was the only time the boss and I had our fingers burned, but we worked it out that overall we had come out even, so there were no complaints ... and we ran a very successful book after that!

My friendship with Mickey began with the card schools at England get-togethers and then we were put together as room-mates. We have similar ideas about football. We both want to play well and we both want to win. And we can talk about life – about other things besides football. We share an interest in horses and pets and we prefer smallish 'lived-in' houses in the country to big flash places in the city.

It's refreshing to meet someone like Mickey in football. There are a lot of players I quite like but would not like to share a room with for one reason or another, but Mickey and I are well suited. We take turns at having lazy days. One day I will order breakfast, collect the papers and generally wait on him and the next day I'll take it easy while he does the work. But when it comes to picking out a couple of horses to back, I usually leave the selection to Mickey.

Life is not always so cosy. After the disappointing return game against Finland, which we won 2–1, Mickey and I decided to go out and share a bottle of wine and talk the match out of our systems. As we walked down Wembley Way we passed groups of stragglers on their way home.

'Where's your white sticks?' shouted one.

'You were crap!' judged another.

'I could have done better than you,' said his mate.

We didn't want sympathy, but we definitely didn't need abuse. We were as sick about the match as they were. I was captain of the side against the Republic of Ireland, and when we walked out at Wembley there seemed to be more Irish fans than English. When we played Finland, 90,000 people came to see us get six or seven goals. It didn't come off and we played badly and they were on our backs after half an hour. That didn't affect me much, but imagine Trevor Francis playing his first game for England against Holland and after twenty-five minutes he hears, 'You're all a load of rubbish!'

I'm a great believer in giving supporters something to cheer about and not taking them for granted, and it is arguable that if we scored a couple of goals early on they would give us tremendous backing. But it was not helpful to cheer the Dutch and boo the English when the teams walked out for the second half. I began to despair of Wembley and wish that the important matches could be played in the north, in Liverpool or Manchester, where they know how to lift a team when it's down. For example, in the first leg of the UEFA Cup Final against Bruges, Liverpool were 2–0 down at Anfield and Bruges were playing brilliantly. Their goals gave them the same kind of confidence that the Dutch showed later at Wembley. But what did the Liverpool supporters do. Did they tell us we were a load of rubbish? No. They knew we needed all the help we could get, and they dragged us back from the dead with their roars of encouragement.

The Poles were crafty in their choice of ground for the World Cup qualifying game against England in 1973. They overlooked Warsaw and took the fixture to Katowice, to a mining community where they knew the football-crazy fans would create a greater volume of support for the team.

With so much at stake, a great deal of psychology is used in football and every advantage should be used to the full. It should be an advantage to play a match at home, and yet the atmosphere at Wembley began to make our most famous stadium seem like a foreign ground to the English players. Instead of the opposition being made to feel that every Englishman in the stadium was after their blood, we began to feel that they were after ours.

A cheer for Ian Callaghan MBE.

A fine body of men ... back row (from left): Joey Jones, John Toshack, Ray Clemence, Phil Thompson, Phil Neal. Middle row: Joe Fagan (coach), Alec Lindsay, David Fairclough, Ray Kennedy, David Johnson, Peter Cormack, Ronnie Moran (trainer). Front: Jimmy Case, Steve Heighway, Ian Callaghan, Bob Paisley, Emlyn Hughes, me, Terry McDermott, plus the UEFA Cup, Charity Shield and League Championship trophy.

Double celebration after winning the UEFA Cup in Bruges, May 1976.

17

The jigsaw puzzle

I have worked out that in the year between January 1976, and January 1977, I travelled 69,790 miles, which amounted to just more than two and three-quarter trips round the world. That included the miles I travelled with the Liverpool and England teams plus the distances I covered for commercial and charity work. It did not include the miles I ran in training and on football grounds from Los Angeles, USA, to Trabzon, Turkey. In the middle of that year my body rebelled.

Having played a season of 58 matches for Liverpool, winning League Championship and UEFA Cup winners' medals, and seven games for England, I returned from the UEFA Cup Final in Bruges and joined the England party to tour America. After that, I began the heat-wave summer by taking a couple of days off and then prepared for the start of England's World Cup qualifying programme with the match in Finland.

Three days after the Finland match I was in the Isle of Man for a couple of days helping to promote fund raising for the Manx Commonwealth Games team. I visited nine schools in four and a half hours, was the guest speaker at a hot-pot supper, refereed a local football match and visited a child in hospital. I had agreed to take part in a match in Paris as part of the celebration of an anniversary of the St Germain club the following Monday, but no sooner had I arrived home from the Isle of Man than London Weekend Television telephoned and asked me to join them in the studio to comment on the European Championship final between Czechoslovakia and West Germany on the Sunday. I was tempted to say 'No', but Mike Smith, the Welsh international team manager, who had also been invited to the studio, offered to drive me to London, and London Weekend had been very good to me in the past. The match dragged on into extra time and was finally settled on penalty kicks. As a result, Mike and I spent almost six hours under the hot lights in the studio.

Next day I played in Paris and began to hear some reaction to my well-publicized thoughts about moving abroad. I had already been told that Barcelona were watching the situation, and a London journalist had telephoned the Liverpool chairman, Mr Smith, and told him that Real Madrid were prepared to make an offer of around £600,000. The chairman said to the journalist, 'I don't want to talk to you. You have no official standing in any way. If Real Madrid want to sign Kevin, or make an offer for Kevin, I want to talk to Real Madrid.' Miljan Miljanic, the Real manager, was at the game in Paris. I think he was keeping an eye on Rob Rensenbrink of Anderlecht as well as myself. We both played and I thought I did quite well. After the match a man approached me and said, 'Mr Miljanic has sent me down. If you are interested in joining Real Madrid, Mr Miljanic would like to talk to you sometime.' I didn't meet Miljanic face to face, but as the team bus was leaving the stadium, he was sitting in a car and he gave me a little wave. I also had a brief chat with Piet Kaizer, the former Ajax star who had become a football agent in Amsterdam and had arranged the match in Paris, and was told that the president of St Germain might be keen to sign me at some future date.

I was asked to stay and play another game in Paris, but I had already committed myself to compete in the television Superstars competition and had promised to open a fête in Rhyl. I was also due to see the Liverpool chairman to discuss the latest developments about the transfer, so I flew from Paris to London at around 7 am the morning after the game, took a train from Euston and arrived in Liverpool at lunchtime.

Jean met me at the station and drove me to Anfield to meet the chairman. Mr Smith told me that he had met representatives of Real Madrid in London and they had told him they were very interested in signing me and asked if they could talk money. The chairman said he didn't really want to talk money until he had discussed it with me and with his board of directors, but he said he would let it be known that Real were interested. He said that although no figure had been mentioned he had assumed they were thinking in terms of about £650,000. He reminded me that I still had two years of my contract to run and said, 'How do you feel?'

'To be honest with you, Mr Chairman,' I said, 'I think it's the chance of a lifetime and I think I should go.'

He said, 'We can't really afford to let you go this year because we're in the European Cup. We don't want to see you go from here. We see you as a future leader of the club.' He continued to give me that kind of build-up but I told him that in spite of what he said a move to Real Madrid was just what I'd been waiting for. It was the challenge I needed and I told the chairman that it would be in the interests of the club as well as mine for me to go.

'Not this year,' he emphasized. 'I'm not even going to talk money with them. I'm not going to discuss it. But if you stay this year, without kicking up a fuss about it, I promise you faithfully that at the end of next season you will go.' That was the best offer I could get and I thought it was fair. We had an agreement and I was determined to do everything I could for the club in the following season.

We talked for an hour and a half, and then Jean drove me home to Wales. We arrived at about 4.30 pm and at 6.15 I was ready to leave for the fête in Rhyl. 'You can't go on like this, you're going to kill yourself,' said Jean, but I had made a promise and I was determined to go. It was a job I was delighted to do, because the fête was in aid of a school for mentally handicapped children. I was also persuaded to visit a local hospital and eventually arrived home at 10.15.

Jean had packed our cases into our Range Rover and she and the dogs were ready for the drive to Bracknell, Berkshire, where I was due to compete in the Superstars competition the following day. We arrived at 4.30 am, I managed to get to bed half-an-hour later – and at 7.45 am I was in the swimming pool, racing in the first heat of the contest. I had withdrawn from the hundred yards sprint because I had injured a leg during the match in Paris and I thought I would have a better chance in the steeplechase, and my progress was fair: third in the swimming, first in the canoeing (pause for lunch), first in the weight-lifting, equal third in the gym exercises, runner-up in the table tennis (pause for a night's sleep), and third in the pistol shooting.

I was in third place overall with two events to go, starting with the cycling. I was riding against Gilbert Van Binst, the Anderlecht captain. Cycling is to Belgium what football is to England, and I noticed he had brought his own bike for the contest. 'Crikey, he must be good,' I thought. 'I'll have to get off to a good start.' I won the draw for the inside lane, and before the race began one of the officials said, 'Don't do anything silly and for God's sake don't let us have any accidents. We've never had any, and we'd like to keep it that way.'

Off we went along the red shale running track, neck and neck down the straight. I was way up out of the saddle, pumping my legs to get extra momentum that would shoot me ahead at the crucial first bend. As the television film revealed only too clearly, I was wobbling all over the track as if the wheels of my bike were buckled. As we came to the bend, Van Binst was only half a wheel up on me and I was convinced I would snatch the lead. Then Van Binst cut across me and his rear wheel touched my front wheel. It was an accident, but while Van Binst rode on, unaware of what had happened, I landed on the ground with a crunch and slid along as the shale shredded my thin vest and skinned my back raw.

Commentators David Vine and Ron Pickering kept repeating that I should go to hospital for an injection, but the stubborn Keegan streak asserted itself again and I insisted on a time trial in order to attempt to win a place in the cycling final. There was a half-hour delay while I was cleaned up and I then raced against the clock and finished second fastest in the heats to win a place in the final against the skier, Franz Klammer, whose big, powerful legs gave him the edge over me. But by finishing second in the cycling I was a point ahead of Ajax star Rudi Krol overall and would win if Krol did not finish ahead of me in the last event, the steeplechase.

My back was so numb I didn't feel pain. As I prepared for the last event Ron Pickering said, 'The six hundred yards steeplechase is a funny race. You can't pace it and finish with a sprint. You've just got to go like hell from the start.' There must have been 5000 youngsters in the crowd and they were all cheering me on because I was the only British competitor. I could hear them screaming my name as I leapt over the hurdles and over the water jumps. The first time I glanced back was when I cleared the last hurdle and saw I was way ahead. I jogged home over the last few yards and collapsed after the finish, but I felt elated. I felt I had proved something by winning the Superstars. I felt I had shown people how fit footballers have to be. Someone asked me, 'What do you think about it?' I said, 'I think I have competed in my first and last Superstars.'

I was told there was still dirt in the wound on my back, so I had a shower and Jean and I went back to our hotel in Ascot. I had won £2800 and I had promised to celebrate with the teenage schoolboys who had helped by carrying my kit. We shared a couple of bottles of champagne and then Jean and I ordered steak and chips. As we ate I told her, 'I think you are going to have to drive home, love, and I think we had better set off because I'm starting to feel a bit ill.'

Jean wanted to take me to hospital there and then but I was keen to return home. Jean had driven about fifteen miles when I said, 'I'll have to go to the back and lie down.' I lay on my stomach at the back of the Range Rover as Jean drove towards the M1. Eventually I couldn't stand the pain any longer. 'You'll have to stop,' I said. I felt as if someone had stuck a knife in my stomach and, not being content with that, was twisting it around.

Jean pulled into the service centre at Newport Pagnell and went over to the police block and said, 'Could you get an ambulance for my husband? He's feeling really bad.' I was still wearing my Superstars gear and a policeman took one look at my bloodied, weeping back and said, 'God, what have you been up to?' An ambulance arrived within five minutes and as I was being taken to Northampton General Hospital I could see Jean following in the Range Rover. I was beginning to have difficulty in breathing and was given oxygen in the ambulance.

When we arrived at hospital and I was waiting to see a doctor someone mentioned to Jean that I might need an operation and, naturally, this upset her. I told her not to worry. Luckily, a good friend, Roger Brown, who works for Mettoy, lived nearby and I said to Jean, 'I'll be OK. Take the dogs to kennels and go to Roger's house. He'll look after you.' Roger was a wonderful help.

I was in hospital for four days and I have never felt so ill. I was on a drip and was given pain-killing injections and the doctor had to give me something to make me sleep. When Jean came to see me on the Sunday I was talking as if it was still Saturday. I had lost a complete day of my life. The doctor said, 'I can't tell you exactly what has been wrong with you, but you've been overdoing things. When you overtax your body, after a while it rejects you somewhere. It could have been your brain or your heart. You are lucky. I put it down to delayed shock from the accident on top of the way you've been running around these past months. Your body is like a car built to do a hundred miles an hour and you've been driving it at a hundred and forty.'

He warned me to take things a bit easier and I promised Jean that I would. But I didn't. I couldn't. For the first time for five years I had been able to lie in a room, look at the ceiling and think and plan. I worried whether or not I would be able to play football again. Then I thought about the holiday in Minorca I had promised Jean – as a belated honeymoon – and how I was supposed to spend a day golfing with the Liverpool lads and had promised to open a leisure centre at Wrexham. All sorts of silly thoughts began to trouble me, and then I realized that I had risked permanent damage to my health and that there was a good chance it would happen again if I allowed things to continue. I had to go abroad, more than ever, to get security without having to lead quite so hectic a life.

I said I would ease up, but there was no use pretending that I could if I wanted to maintain the standard of living to which I had grown accustomed. I had to be out and about working at the commercial side, because the money I earned from English football alone was not enough. I had contracts to fulfil. It was impossible for me to sit back . . . and Liverpool were about to start the season that built into an amazing quest for 'The Treble' – the League Championship, FA Cup and European Cup.

It was not long before my evenings at home were being punctuated by the almost

Apeing in Los Angeles.

Cycle crash in the Superstars contest.

persistent ringing of the telephone, as Club representatives and agents from abroad came through with offers, hints of offers or reminders of offers. I spoke to a representative of Real Madrid several times. A chap from Brussels contacted me around the time Liverpool played Crusaders, of Belfast, in the first round of the European Cup and said, 'Bayern Munich are interested – do you think your club would settle for a fee of around £400,000 to £450,000?' I tried to explain that they had turned down a possible £650,000 from Real Madrid, so they were hardly likely to take £200,000 less at that stage. But I made sure not to close any doors on myself. There was a call from a fellow in Denmark who said he represented Borussia Dortmund. He repeated what others had said: 'Do you think they will reduce the fee they want for you?'

I walked out of Anfield five minutes before the team coach was due to leave for West Bromwich, where we were beaten in a replay in the second round of the League Cup on 6 September, and a man came up to me and said, 'Mr Keegan, my name is Felix. I am from Brussels.' He handed me his card, which described him as a football agent. I said I could talk to him for two minutes and no longer. 'I have been asked by a German club to see if you would be willing to go there.' Felix turned out to be the man who had telephoned from Brussels. He was acting for Bayern Munich, and, after introducing himself, he kept in touch. Like most of my foreign callers, he always seemed to ring late at night.

After listening to what the agents had to say, my reply was always the same. They would have to speak to the Liverpool chairman, and the chairman would insist that any negotiations were done between the clubs, the English way, not through agents, as is the custom on the Continent.

When I was in London with the England squad for the game against Finland at Wembley in October there was a sinister episode back home in Wales that added to my eagerness to make the break and try something new. I had already put extra pressure on my professional life by becoming the centre of European transfer speculation and having to keep as high a level of consistency as possible so that potential buyers would not lose interest. Then, suddenly, Jean's peace of mind was shattered.

The police arrived at the house while I was away. At first Jean thought it was a social call, because we knew the local policemen well. But it turned out that they had been sent to protect Jean because an anonymous caller to *The Sun* had said he had overheard some Irishmen planning to kidnap her and demand a £40,000 ransom. Fortunately, Jean's parents were staying with us at the time, otherwise she would have been in an even worse state of nerves. The police guarded the house around the clock in shifts and Jean decided not to tell me about the threat until I returned from London.

It seemed like a false alarm until a transit van was spotted coming up the drive. Instead of stopping on the forecourt, which would have been normal, the van was driven right up to the back door of the house. The police told Jean and her parents to lie on the lounge floor and an officer went to the door and showed his face to the caller, keeping his uniform hidden from view. A man with a strong Irish accent asked if we had any antiques. He was told we hadn't. He didn't patter on the way dealers usually do. He just asked where the road at the bottom of the lane came from and went to. That seemed an odd question, because he had diverted from the Mold – St Asaph road where the signpost showed clearly, 'Cilcain'. It seemed strange that he had by-passed the house at the bottom of the lane and chosen to drive to ours. When he reversed his van and drove away, other men could be seen through the back window of the vehicle. Instead of driving back to the main road, the van turned right and was followed and stopped by a police patrol car. The driver said he was an antique dealer from Birmingham, though his companions left little room for antiques in the van. The police checked his story and found it to be true.

Jean became unsettled after that affair. She was no longer reluctant to sell the house and, though we both loved the country life and the people around us, we decided she would feel more secure in an area where houses and neighbours were situated more closely together.

Piet Kaizer came to Liverpool to see me shortly after the Finland game. We had a meal together and he told me a lot of interesting things about club football in Europe. He then showed me a contract and said, 'Read over it and see what you think.' It amounted to an agreement for him to act on my behalf in negotiations with foreign clubs. He mentioned Barcelona and said if Cruyff decided to move he could do a deal for me there. I had already had a similar proposition from an agent in England. I said I would take the contract home and think about it, but I wasn't interested in tying myself to any agent at that stage. It was not that I didn't trust them. It was more a case of not wanting to commit myself or place myself entirely into the hands of a third party. I didn't want to be a dummy, told to 'Come here, come there, come everywhere.'

A few days after my meeting with Kaizer, Liverpool travelled to Turkey to play Trabzonspor in the second round of the European Cup. I have been to some austere places, but that beat them all. Our hotel was like a YMCA building, with no disrespect to the YMCA. A double room with breakfast cost four pounds a night so, with the cost of living being similar to that in Britain, we were hardly in the lap of luxury. The only highlight of that dreadful trip for me was when Mr Smith asked me to see him in his room and gave me the details of an offer from Juventus, of Turin.

The Italians had talked in terms of a million-pound deal. 'The beauty is that they don't want you for two years because Italy's ban on foreign players won't be lifted until then,' he said. We laughed, because I would be pushing twenty-eight by then, and though the Italians believe their players are in their prime at that age I would probably have played enough games to have pushed me to the top of the hill. 'The advantages would be that you could play for England if they qualify for Argentina; Juventus are willing to pay you wages on top of what you earn from Liverpool during the two years before you actually play for them and they are also willing to put you in charge of a Fiat agency.'

Although Liverpool had not gone into detail about the actual amounts involved, they were prepared to talk to Juventus when England played in Rome in November. I told Mr Smith, 'To be honest, Italy would be my last choice. I don't want to go to Italy – but I'm not going to say that to them. I want to know exactly what would be involved.' I was not keen on the idea of waiting for two years, because the reason I wanted a move was that I needed a change immediately. I didn't fancy running an agency for Fiat, who sponsor Juventus, because that would have been an additional worry and would probably have been more to their advantage than mine. Surely my attitude to what could have been the most lucrative move proved that I was not only interested in money.

Mr Smith and the Liverpool secretary, Peter Robinson, travelled to Italy, but I didn't play well. I was so tightly marked that Juventus must have wondered if I was on the field. After that performance I didn't even ask the chairman how their talks had gone. I thought Juventus's interest might have wavered.

I began to think that my performances for England during the season might have made interested foreign clubs look elsewhere, but then I reasoned that any clubs who were prepared to talk to Liverpool in such enormous financial terms must have seen enough of me at club level to know what I could do. In fact I was told that Juventus had made further inquiries, but the two-year wait was always a stumbling block to that deal.

There was a tentative approach from New York Cosmos. Although I felt I was a bit too young to leave the established European game, I was intrigued by the challenge of America, where Pele had done such a marvellous job, and playing for New York would have involved a great deal of public relations work as well as football. We did not get down to deep discussion, but perhaps one day we shall.

All other considerations were reduced to nothing on 4 December, when Dad died. I was playing for Liverpool at Ipswich and it was decided not to break the news to me until after the match, but I sensed what had happened when my brother, Mike, did not show up with Dad's pal, Harry Wadsley, as usual. Liverpool lost 1–0 and the drive to Doncaster afterwards was terrible. I thought that journey would never end, and my mind was filled with thoughts of Dad and the times we'd had. The last time I saw him I had trimmed his hair and had told him he was becoming too trendy. Before he died, Dad asked Mum for the result of the match. 'I know they lost but I don't know by how many,' he said. 'No,' said Mum. 'They've won 2–0 with goals by Toshack and Keegan.' I tried to be realistic and not to show my feelings, especially when I saw how upset everyone else was at home, but when Dad died a part of me died, too. I played football for Dad and it could never be quite the same again. During the funeral I saw a familiar face. David Anderson, my boyhood pal from Spring Gardens, was driving the hearse.

While we were preparing for the funeral we had a telephone call to say that Jean's horse, Danny, had been killed. How that happened is still a mystery. Danny was so friendly and trusting. We had left him in the care of our good friend, Jim Palin, from whom we had bought him, and one day, when the snow was thick on the fields, Danny was missing. After a long search, Jim found him. The snow had hidden the body, and at first, when he saw Danny's head, Jim thought he had been shot between the eyes. The police were called, and after an examination by a vet it was concluded that death had probably been caused by Danny running into a rock or some other solid object. We had to accept that there was no evidence of foul play, but we couldn't help wondering, in view of the fact that both Jean and I had been threatened.

There were occasions, I must confess, when I became depressed even though Liverpool were challenging strongly for three trophies. Apart from an amazing 5–1 defeat at Aston Villa, our League form was consistent with that of champions, but I was no longer enjoying the games as I should. Perhaps I was still affected by Dad's death, but when I injured my shoulder by charging Stoke City goalkeeper Peter Shilton and was ruled out of the most important match of Boxing Day Monday, at Manchester City, I felt no sense of loss. For the first time in my career I was not upset about having to miss a game. I wished my future had been decided.

Mr Smith arranged for me to meet a friend of his, Les Connor, who advised me about financial matters and the pitfalls of earning money abroad. I gave him a breakdown of my earnings and potential earnings in England and stressed that I mainly wanted the move in order to fulfil an ambition and if that meant having to deposit money in Switzerland, or even having to live there one day, I was adaptable enough to do that. The chairman told me he had heard nothing from Barcelona, but that didn't surprise me, because they still had Cruyff and Neeskens and wanted them to sign new contracts, so they weren't going to push too hard. It was my impression that Barcelona regarded me as a sort of stand-by and I was more keen to go to Real Madrid if the move was to be to Spain.

Before Liverpool's game against Birmingham City at Anfield on 5 February, the chairman said, 'I must have a chat with you afterwards.' We won 4–1 and then Mr Smith told me the club had received a written offer from Real Madrid. He didn't mention the size of Real's offer but said he had told them he would let them know within a month. I missed the away leg of the European Cup quarter final against St Etienne because of an injury, but the lads played well and were unlucky to concede a goal. I was fit for the return game, which was a classic, and Liverpool won 3–1. Between then, 16 March, and the first leg of the European Cup semi-final in Zurich, on 6 April, Felix from Brussels telephoned to say that Bayern Munich were still keen to sign me.

Even though we were having to press on without Phil Thompson, Ian Callaghan and John Toshack, who had all been seriously injured, we were far too strong for Zurich and beat them 3–1 in the first leg in spite of conceding a penalty early in the game. We were amazed at the ease with which we won that game, and we coasted through the second leg to win 3–0. While in Zurich I met Gunther Netzer, who had left Real and was playing for the local Grasshoppers club. I told him Real and Bayern were interested in me and he said, 'Go to Real Madrid. It's the greatest club in the world.'

Any chance of taking Netzer's advice ended when Real decided they had to make a move and could no longer wait for Liverpool to accept their offer. They paid £450,000 to Borussia Monchengladbach, our European Cup Final opponents, for Ulrich Stielike, who would team up with the former Borussia player Henning Jensen, the Dane, as the pair of foreign players Real were allowed under Spanish rules. I had balanced the merits of a move to Madrid or Munich, and, quite honestly, either would have pleased me. Now it seemed to be Bayern or nowhere.

The chairman, who had dealt with the whole business, had been fair and open with me in all our talks. Now, with Bayern having made a reported £500,000 from the sale of Beckenbauer to New York Cosmos (Beckenbauer is said to have been paid a million pounds), and having contacted Liverpool again, I thought it was time to remind him about his promise to me. On 5 May I told him that if he didn't keep his word I would quit. Liverpool were within sight of the League title, had beaten Everton after two tight games in the FA Cup semi-final and were due to play Manchester United in the Final and would go from Wembley to Rome for the European Final. The season was running out and my patience was running short, though I knew Liverpool were hoping to receive an offer closer to their valuation.

On 14 May Liverpool retained the championship with a goalless draw at Anfield against West Ham United, who desperately needed the point to avoid relegation. That was my last competitive match for Liverpool at Anfield and, though the game was something of an anti-climax, the fans celebrated with their usual volume of noise. I wanted to run around the ground with the other lads to show off the trophy, but some of the fans invaded the pitch and spoiled that idea, so I stayed in the centre of the field with Phil Thompson and John Toshack, who missed the game because of injuries. With the championship trophy back upstairs at Anfield, the 'treble' was within reach and my future was beginning to take shape. S.V. Hamburg, winners of the European Cup-winners' Cup, set up a meeting with Mr Smith (through my old friend Felix) on the eve of the FA Cup Final on 21 May against Manchester United. Meanwhile, Stielike's transfer to Madrid was interrupted by the West German Football Federation, who decided to hold him to a declaration he had signed promising not to leave the country until after the World Cup Finals in Argentina. Mr Smith told Hamburg he would not discuss a fee until after the European Cup Final the following Wednesday 25 May, and I hoped Real Madrid would not come back in with an offer, because by this time I fancied West German football more.

Liverpool did not manage to put things together at Wembley but were still the better team. The all-important breaks fell to United in the second half and they won 2–1. That was the end of the treble, but I believe we sacrificed the FA Cup for the most important trophy of all. I do not think we would have played with as much determination in Rome against Borussia Mönchengladbach if we had beaten United. I think we would have been too relaxed. Borussia retained the West German championship on the weekend before the final in Rome, but that triumph failed to give them the impetus to withstand our pressure.

That night in Rome when I played my last game for Liverpool will live with me forever. I went into the match knowing that Mr Smith had arranged to go to Hamburg the following weekend and that the eyes of Europe would be upon me. It was a tremendous challenge and thankfully I was able to respond to it, even though I was marked 'man-for-man' by Berti Vogts, one of the most accomplished defenders in the world. Berti tried to be my second skin, but I managed to get the edge over him and helped Liverpool to win 3–1. The Liverpool fans made Rome their own and turned the Olympic stadium into Anfield, making us feel we were playing a home match. Terry McDermott gave us the lead in the first half and, even though Allan Simonsen took advantage of a bad back pass to score a fine equalizing goal, we had the confidence and ability to come back strongly. Tommy Smith scored with a cracking header – his first goal of the season in his six hundredth game for Liverpool – and Phil Neal scored our third goal from the penalty spot after Vogts brought me down in the penalty box.

I felt good. I knew my game had fallen into place again and that the last piece in

ABOVE Arriving in Rome for the European Cup final.

LEFT Mission accomplished! The return flight with Jean.

the jigsaw puzzle would soon be put in place. I knew my transfer form was as good as signed. I felt that my allegiance to Liverpool was over; especially my allegiance to a certain section of the supporters, who had shown themselves to be human – just as fickle as fans everywhere. The way they turned against me during the last couple of months of the season, when I had lost my consistency and needed their support, proved to me that it was right for me to go. My name was chanted in Rome, when I played well again, but I had barely heard the supporters for a year. To be honest, I found it hard to forget that as I waved to them at the Olympic Stadium. It was good to see that Shanks was with the official party at the Holiday Inn this time, remembering how badly he was treated the previous year in Bruges. Mum was also at the reception – and Berti Vogts dropped in to congratulate us and to ask me if I would like to play for Borussia. My mind was made up. I wanted to go to Hamburg, the club which had wanted me at a time when my form had faltered. They had believed in me and I believed in them.

The following Sunday I travelled to Hamburg for a medical examination and to have a look around with Jean, and in London the next Friday, 3 June, the deal was finalized. My wait was over. I signed a contract for two years with Hamburg, having a further one-year option and the terms for this were more than fair. On this day, when I shook hands with Bob Paisley and John Smith, I felt sad for the first time in the whole year. I am not a soft or emotional person, but for the first time I began to realize what I would be leaving behind. The chairman and I had proved to be men of our word and I only hope any other transfer in which I may be involved goes through as smoothly and with as much honesty. At the time of leaving I had no plans to return. My only concern was to play well in Germany and to continue to win as many honours as possible.

So many people had advised me, and I had listened to what they had to say. But the decision had to be mine, and I was pleased I had had the confidence to make the move. If I failed I could not blame anyone except myself, and that summed up the first twenty-six years of my life. If I had acted on some of the advice I was given I would not be where I am today. I managed to retain the same streak of independence I had when I kicked a ball against Mrs Wild's wall in Spring Gardens as a small boy. I am grateful that I had the talent to do what I wanted to do with my life. I was late for my trial at Doncaster Rovers and Coventry City turned me down. But perhaps it was good to have had a few disappointments on the way.